BRING THE FAMILY
TOGETHER FOR
RED LETTER ADVENT!

DOWNLOAD THE FREE

ADVENT CHALLENGE
Family Addition

GRAB THIS FREE RESOURCE AT
WWW.REDLETTERADVENT.COM/RESOURCES

TABLE OF
CONT

ENTS

BEFORE YOU BEGIN

Here are a few helpful tips to maximize this 25-Day Challenge.

Invite someone to join with you. The most significant challenges you conquer are not meant to be tackled alone. We hope you will read this book with at least one other person. If you are participating in *Red Letter Advent* with your small group or church, try to find one person to hold you accountable for the next 25 days. That person should be someone you trust, who walks as a disciple of Jesus. Identify specifics and parameters of the partnership, such as how often you check in with one another and what questions you ask each other at those check-ins.

Complete the daily challenges. Each of the daily readings offers a challenge to complete. To get the most out of this book, take on the challenges. Some have an inner, thoughtful focus, while others have an external, serving aspect. For an internal challenge, take time with the questions. Be honest with your reflections and write down your responses. When it is an external challenge, try your best to complete the challenge, even if it means modifying it to match your ability.

On certain days, you'll find optional challenges. These are activities that may require more time or resources and may not be feasible to complete in a single day. Some may involve a financial cost. However, they offer a unique and enriching experience to enhance your Advent celebration.

Don't give up. This challenge goes beyond checking boxes just to get it done. It allows you to put your beliefs into action. If you miss a day or struggle to complete a day, don't give up. Instead, give yourself grace and pick up the next day. Keep going. We know the Christmas season is crazy, so don't put too much pressure on yourself or make it another to-do checklist. Know that even if you just complete one, that's one more than none.

Share the wins. Join the thousands of others embarking on the journey. Use #RedLetterAdvent on social media to share pictures, quotes, stories, or testimonies of what God is doing. Sharing your wins publicly will not only encourage others to do the same, but it will also give people the opportunity to glorify God through your witness.

ABOUT
THE AUTHORS

Zach Zehnder is a husband, father, pastor, public speaker, and author. He is the Founder and President of Red Letter Living, author of the bestselling *Red Letter Challenge* book, and host of the podcast *The Red Letter Disciple*. He serves as a teaching pastor at King of Kings in Omaha, NE.

Allison Zehnder grew up as a missionary kid in Togo, West Africa. After moving back to the United States, she graduated from Concordia University Wisconsin with a degree in Theology and minors in Missions and Youth Ministry. She co-authored four kids books in the *Red Letter Challenge* series and writes for Red Letter Living.

For more on this husband-and-wife team, to book Zach as a speaker, or to check out their other books and projects, go to **www.redletterchallenge.com**.

Allison and I have worked on many projects in tandem, but this was our first joint effort. We divided the weeks, each taking half the days to be responsible for creatively. Since this is our first project writing simultaneously, it took some thought to create one unified voice with two different writers. Although we worked hard to edit it into one seamless voice, we also see value in hearing from both of us individually. We used first-person narrative for some of our daily devotions so you need to know which one of us you are hearing from. You will see these two different doodles in front of the sections for which we were creatively responsible.

INTRODUCTION

"MY SHEEP LISTEN TO MY VOICE; I KNOW THEM, AND THEY FOLLOW ME," JOHN 10:27.

THE UNBOXING EXPERIENCE

 It's fun to unbox things. In the world of technology, Apple popularized the term unboxing and made it an entire experience. They understood the importance of prolonging the thrill when their customers received a beautifully wrapped device.

I remember opening my first iPhone and marveling at the sleek box and how all the components were perfectly wrapped and positioned. Apple created beautiful products, and their incredible packaging left me in awe. Not only was there a gorgeous design to the box, but Apple wanted to eliminate any friction as you open one of their products. The process is as easy as possible. Every accessory has a perfectly molded, plastic space allotted to it, and it ends when you remove the thin protective screen covering and the device is in your hands. While this process may have been effortless for you, it was difficult for Apple.

Before the first iPhone came out in 2007, Apple filed over two hundred patents, including a patent for the box itself. Even CEO Steve Jobs spent countless hours involved in the packaging. Adam Lashinsky, the author of *Inside Apple*, claimed that only a few individuals can access a secret packaging room at Apple headquarters. Months before the first iPhone's release, Apple hired a packaging designer whose sole job was to open boxes. In summary, everything you experience when you unbox an Apple iPhone is intentional.

THE UNBOXING OF A GIFT MATTERS.

THE GREATEST GIFT

Christmas is the day we celebrate God sending his Son to save the world. It marks when Jesus would step down into humanity to be the greatest gift the world has ever known. His arrival on earth offers every person the gift of grace and eternal life.

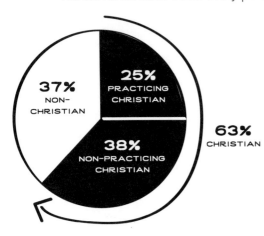

This news should have everyone anxious to rip open this gift. Many have received this gift already. In 2021, Pew Research claimed that 63% of Americans still professed a belief in Jesus.[1] That's a higher number than I would have expected. But the statistic gets more sobering once you dig deeper into people's actual living out of this belief. Barna's research claims that only 25% of Americans are now practicing Christians.[2]

There should be a difference between believing and practicing.

When Jesus came to earth, a similar pattern emerged. People believed in him, but that belief didn't automatically mean they followed him. John Mark Comer, the author of *Practicing the Way*, said, "Tens of thousands of people were drawn to Jesus, but only a few hundred at most became his apprentices*."[3] *Comer's word for disciple.

According to Comer, after being offered the chance of a lifetime, most people mentioned in the four gospels said "no thanks" to the gift.

Let's pause to do some math.

If roughly 37% do not believe in Jesus and another 38% of people are not practicing Christians, that means that 75% of people in the United States have no idea what to do with Jesus. Three out of four people may have received the gift but haven't unboxed Jesus. What a tragedy!

Another way to sum it up could be:

AFTER BEING GIVEN THE GIFT OF GRACE, MOST PEOPLE REMOVE THE WRAPPING BUT LEAVE JESUS IN THE BOX.

These statistics reveal a gap between a person believing in Jesus and living out their faith as a disciple. People receive salvation easily. It gives them confidence in their eternity. But after that, they leave Jesus in the box, all wrapped up. There is much more to the gift God has for you than just an entry into heaven.

The gift of Jesus allows you to live a meaningful life right now—a life that follows after him. Jesus's invitation was not just to believe but to follow him. More than 26 times in the Gospels, Jesus says, **"Follow me."**

To experience Christmas is to respond to God's gift of salvation by saying, "Yes, I believe." But receiving is not just a declaration; it's multiplying these gifts every day of your life. It's in believing *and* following that we truly unbox the gift of Jesus.

So, I invite you to come on a 25-day journey as we unbox what Christmas is all about.

THE 25-DAY ADVENT UNBOXING

This devotional compares the Advent season to the online shopping experience. Here's how our journey will look:

DAY 1: You will explore what Advent is all about. I'll introduce you to four gifts you'll be unboxing: hope, peace, joy, and love. People have celebrated these four gifts during Advent for centuries. During *Red Letter Advent*, you will not only unbox God's gifts, but learn how to put them into practice as well.

HOPE
DAYS 2-7

PEACE
DAYS 8-13

JOY
DAYS 14-19

LOVE
DAYS 20-25

In each gift, we will take you through six unboxing stages. Like purchasing an item or a gift online, here are those steps in order:

ADD TO CART   CHECKOUT   IN TRANSIT   HANDLE WITH CARE   DELIVERED   RETURNS

Here's what you can expect as you unbox hope, peace, joy, and love from Days 2 to 25.

STAGE 1: ADD TO CART (DAYS 2, 8, 14, 20)

It's easy and free to add things to your cart. While we can add many good things to our lives, not everything is best. Sometimes, our life carts feel heavy because we have added too much unnecessary baggage. In the Add to Cart Stage of each gift, the challenge will be to identify what you are currently adding to your cart of life and whether it's helpful or harmful.

STAGE 2: CHECKOUT (DAYS 3, 9, 15, 21)

Once you add a gift to your cart, it's time to checkout and select payment. Every gift has a cost. It's tempting to want to try to earn our gifts, but earning a gift makes it not a gift anymore. Still, it takes time to accept something with no strings attached. In the Checkout Stage, you will learn the valuable price Jesus paid for hope, peace, joy, and love. We will challenge you to receive these gifts of God, not with your payment, but through Jesus's sacrifice.

STAGE 3: IN TRANSIT (DAYS 4, 10, 16, 22)

The gift has been paid for and is on its way. Now you are in full wait mode. While you wait, one of the best things you can do is prepare to receive the gift. Some gifts require more preparation than others. The gifts of hope, peace, joy, and love are not small. So, during the In Transit Stage, we will challenge you to practice disciplines and habits that will prepare you to receive what God has in store for you.

STAGE 4: HANDLE WITH CARE (DAYS 5, 11, 17, 23)

Although Christmas brings joyful anticipation and causes for celebration, you live in a world filled with brokenness. For some, this world's painful and broken parts overshadow the season. We need to remember to handle those people with care and concern. The Handle with Care Stage challenges will help you reflect on how sin and brokenness keep you or others from experiencing hope, joy, peace, and love.

STAGE 5: DELIVERED (DAYS 6, 12, 18, 24)

The moment has finally arrived! The gifts of hope, peace, joy, and love are available. These presents aren't fairytales or temporary fixes. They are permanent treasures from God that he wants you to rip open and experience. During the Delivered Stage, you will be encouraged to express gratitude and acknowledge how these gifts make a difference in your life today and in the lives of others as you share them.

STAGE 6: RETURNS (DAYS 7, 13, 19, 25)

Not only do you receive these gifts, but God then asks you to share them with others. Like an investment return that multiplies and grows, everyone wins when we give away, or return, what God gives to us to someone else. The return is the multiplication of the gift given to us. In the Returns Stage, we will challenge you to give away hope, peace, joy, and love to those who need them most.

DECLARE WITH YOUR MOUTH

One last thing: if you are new to Christianity and have never received this gift of grace, I want to let you know it's here for you. You don't have to wait until Christmas to open it. The Bible says that all you need to do to receive this gift is to believe in Jesus as your Savior and Lord.

"IF YOU DECLARE WITH YOUR MOUTH, 'JESUS IS LORD,' AND BELIEVE IN YOUR HEART THAT GOD RAISED HIM FROM THE DEAD, YOU WILL BE SAVED. FOR IT IS WITH YOUR HEART THAT YOU BELIEVE AND ARE JUSTIFIED, AND IT IS WITH YOUR MOUTH THAT YOU PROFESS YOUR FAITH AND ARE SAVED" (ROMANS 10:9-10).

I hope you experience the hope, peace, joy, and love of Jesus as you unbox the gifts God has prepared for you this Advent Season.

DAY 1
WHAT IS ADVENT?

"FOR TO US A CHILD IS BORN, TO US A SON IS GIVEN; AND THE GOVERNMENT SHALL BE UPON HIS SHOULDER, AND HIS NAME SHALL BE CALLED WONDERFUL COUNSELOR, MIGHTY GOD, EVERLASTING FATHER, PRINCE OF PEACE" (ISAIAH 9:6).

CRAZY TRADITIONS

Everything changes at Christmastime. We change what we say, what our house looks like, what we wear, what we listen to, and what our buying patterns are. In 2021, Christmas passed the one trillion-dollar industry mark in the United States. The average American adult now spends more than a thousand dollars on gifts alone!

Now that my kids are both teenagers, I'm ready to abandon some family holiday traditions. One I am glad to be done with is hiding the Elf on the Shelf. One Christmas, two families each gifted us an Elf on the Shelf. Double the fun, right?!? If you are unfamiliar with the Elf on the Shelf tradition, it is a toy that came out in 2005. Each elf doll comes with a storybook about the elf. The tradition that went along with the doll was that the elf arrived at your home on December 1 and was the go-between for Santa. After taking note of good and bad behavior, he reported back to the North Pole. The most critical warning about the elf is that you cannot touch him, or he will lose his magic. (FYI: It is not exactly a gospel-centered message.)

The first thing you do with an elf is give them a name, so our elves are named Frank and Snowball. Each morning until Christmas, Frank and Snowball were moved to a different location around our house. The fun part of this tradition was our kids trying to find where we hid the elves every morning. The not-so-fun part was Allison and I stumbling around hiding our elves at 4 AM in the dark because we forgot to hide them the night before.

It is hard to break a tradition once it's started, but thankfully, our boys are older now. Frank and Snowball don't move anymore, but there are still many crazy Christmas traditions we keep up every December. Between hanging lights, decorating the house, attending ugly sweater and staff Christmas parties, decorating Christmas cookies, mailing Christmas cards, watching Christmas movies, buying Christmas presents, and writing letters to Santa, it feels like too much!

Before you start calling me Ebenezer Scrooge, I love most Christmas traditions. (Well, except for eating fruitcake.) The pageantry, parties, and punch of the season can be joy-filled. But amid all these other traditions, we must remember the point of Christmas. **Christmas is the day we celebrate God's coming to save humanity.**

JESUS ONCE SAID, "FOR WHERE YOUR TREASURE IS, THERE YOUR HEART WILL BE ALSO" (LUKE 12:34).

If you are the average American adult, your treasure and your heart get wrapped up in keeping so many Christmas traditions alive. I'm not here to remove traditions; please get in the Christmas spirit. But I want you to remember what this day is all about. One way to ensure you get it is to celebrate Advent.

MORE THAN CHOCOLATE

Due to the popularization of Advent calendars, most people are familiar with the word Advent. It's great that Advent calendars have become trendy! I love it when culture adopts Christian traditions because it means we are doing something right. But we have to make sure people understand what these meaningful traditions are all about. We don't want them to take the fun and miss out on its purpose. Unfortunately, a lot of Christians don't even know where Advent started. It didn't start with chocolate countdowns. It originally began as a Christian season.

The celebration of Advent is relatively new in our history, and it's important to remember that Jesus didn't celebrate Advent. The disciples would not have ever talked about Advent. There is no mention of it in the Bible. Does that mean it's wrong to celebrate it? Not at all!

Advent comes from the Latin Word *adventus,* which means coming. Every year, the season of Advent prepares you for the coming of Jesus on Christmas Day.

Advent began showing up in the church year calendar around the start of the 5th century. It included the four Sundays before Christmas. Advent hymns started around the 1500s, beginning with the famous hymn *O Come O Come Emmanuel* from France. Then, in 1839, a German pastor from Hamburg named Johann Hinrich Wichern took a wagon wheel and used it to make the first Advent wreath. Tradition has it that he used four red candles to represent the four Sundays and twenty little white candles to represent each day of the week in between. And so, Advent and its wreath traditions were born.

Our church has an Advent wreath. Unlike Wichern's wreath, it has only four candles, representing the four weeks of Advent. We light candles consecutively each Sunday until all four shine on Christmas. (The dates of those Sundays change yearly, so many people begin Advent on December 1 rather than the first Sunday.)

Instead of red, three of the four candles (the first, second, and fourth) are purple because violet signifies a time of prayer, penance, and sacrifice. The third candle is pink and symbolizes joy. It may look like a mismatched candle set, but that pink candle is intentional—I promise! Our family uses an Advent wreath at home as well. We also used Advent calendars with our boys when they were younger as a daily countdown to the coming of Jesus.

The first Advent calendars were made of paper. Today, you can find 25-day Christmas countdowns with nearly anything inside. Search "Advent calendar" in Google, and you'll discover countdowns filled with candy, candles, LEGO, jewelry, action figures, tea bags, makeup, and even beer or wine. Again, I love it when the secular world borrows Christian things. But, when people do more than participate and genuinely understand the tradition in its first place, it makes it that much more meaningful.

While Advent isn't in the Bible, waiting for a Savior began in the Garden of Eden. The Israelites in the Old Testament knew all about waiting for a Messiah to arrive. Isaiah, the prophet, wrote about a child being born and worshiped.

"FOR TO US A CHILD IS BORN, TO US A SON IS GIVEN; AND THE GOVERNMENT SHALL BE UPON HIS SHOULDER, AND HIS NAME SHALL BE CALLED WONDERFUL COUNSELOR, MIGHTY GOD, EVERLASTING FATHER, PRINCE OF PEACE" (ISAIAH 9:6).

For the Israelites, Advent was much longer than twenty-five days. And there was no chocolate waiting for them each day. Their waiting period lasted for thousands of years.

Would the Savior ever come? The people wondered. *When will this waiting finally be over?*

NOW AND NOT YET

Jesus came and changed the world on Christmas morning. So, if Jesus came already, why is Advent, or waiting, still even a thing?

After Jesus accomplished his rescue mission, before he ascended back to heaven, he promised would return yet again.

So here we are, roughly 2000 years into this new season of "adventing". We are still waiting, preparing, and feeling excited about the second coming of Christ. Theologians call this period we live in the "Now and Not Yet." Jesus came and brought grace to all, so we now have access to his kingdom. That's why we can unbox gifts like hope, peace, joy, and love today. These things will keep us going until Christ's second coming. But, you could make the case that every day is Advent because Christians continually wait for Jesus to return. Here's the good news: even though you are waiting, you can still thrive in the now. Not only that, but you can also anticipate a not-yet future that will blow away even the best of what you might experience today! So, Advent is a time to look back at what God has done at his first coming on Christmas morning *and* to look forward to his coming again. This Now and Not Yet Period helps you wait well in the middle.

WAITING WELL

So, how exactly do you wait well? One way is to bring the light.

When someone arrives at your house, you turn on the lights for your guest. During the winter, when there is more darkness than light, candles are a way to celebrate Jesus as the world's light. For centuries, Christians worldwide have focused on bringing the light to others while they waited. This tradition has grown into one that you can continue.

The four candles lit each Sunday represent Jesus's gifts he gave you. The gifts they have come to represent are hope, peace, joy, and love. Christians can also be lights in a dark world. But we don't just hand people candles. We extend what they represent.

I hope you participate in some fun traditions this Christmas season (and even great hiding places for your elf!) But, most importantly, I pray Jesus's coming highlight of everything you experience this season.

GET READY TO UNBOX YOUR GIFTS.

CHALLENGE DAY 1
ADD TO CART

Get in the Christmas spirit. Read the Christmas story from Luke 2:1-21 and answer the following questions.

Of the four gifts of Advent, hope, peace, joy, and love, which do you need the most right now? Why did you choose this gift?

_____

_____

_____

OPTIONAL CHALLENGE

Begin the tradition of an Advent wreath in your home. Get a wreath with four candles and light them leading up to Christmas. Remember, it doesn't have to be a fancy one. Make one yourself! The tradition is to light one candle during the first week, two during the second week, etc. until you light all four candles. You can join together as a family, offer daily prayers, and share verses from the Bible as you light these candles.

"IN HIS NAME THE NATIONS WILL PUT THEIR HOPE."

MATTHEW 12:21

WEEK OF

HOPE

DAY 2

HOPE:

ADD
TO CART

"AND ALL WHO HEARD IT WERE AMAZED AT WHAT THE SHEPHERDS SAID TO THEM" (LUKE 2:18).

MY GREATEST HOPE

The first stage of unboxing is Add to Cart. You add many good things to your cart of life. Even if they aren't bad things, it doesn't mean they are the best things for you. Your life's cart may feel cramped because you have added too many unnecessary things. Today, we want to challenge you to think about how you experience or look for hope in the world. What fills you with hope this Advent season? During World War II, many people were looking for hope.

One was a young Jewish teenage girl who went into hiding. For two and a half years Anne Frank and her family remained hidden behind a wall to escape Nazi Germany. Through her diary, we read what a thirteen-year-old girl hoped for while they hid. Some of the things she wished for were things we take for granted every day, like seeing the sky, feeling the rain or sunshine, lying on the grass, or walking. Other things she hoped for were specific to a young woman, such as buying toiletries like "lipstick, eyebrow pencil, bath salts, bath powder, eau-de-Cologne, soap, and a powder puff."[4]

But above all these things, she hoped to be a writer. Read the excerpt from her diary below.

> "I can shake off everything if I write; my sorrows disappear, my courage is reborn. But, and that is the greatest question, will I ever be able to write anything great, will I ever become a journalist or a writer? I hope so, oh, I hope so very much, for I can recapture everything when I write, my thoughts, my ideas and my fantasies."[5]

Before discussing everything people add to their cart looking for hope, I want to establish what I mean by saying hope. Anne used hope to capture her strong wish, intent, or aspiration for certain things to happen. You may have said similar phrases to the following:

* You hope it won't rain during the party.

* You hope your college degree will get you a job in a particular career.

* You hope somebody has an engagement ring under the tree with your name on it.

While these hopes express a natural longing for something, it doesn't indicate any probability of it happening. You hoping for it doesn't mean it will.

* It does rain at parties.

* Over half of college graduates work a job outside their field.[6]

* Little boxes can contain chocolate instead of a diamond.

In this context, hope is just wishful thinking.

THE ROPE HOPE

In the Bible, hope means something much bigger than wishful thinking. The word hope in the New Testament comes from the Greek word *elpis*, meaning "expectation, trust, and confidence." It comes from the root word *elpo*, which means "anticipating with pleasure and welcoming."

Now, examine the Old Testament's use of the word hope. The Hebrew word for hope is *tikvah*. *Tikvah* means a sure, strong rope—something steady and dependable to count on. Hope is an expectation of what is guaranteed.

When we looked at biblical words for hope, we realized that the authors weren't talking about wishful thinking. They meant hope beyond just wanting something, like a beautiful gift or good weather. Biblical hope combined desire with absolute assurance of that thing coming to reality.

The hope of the Bible is as much about the guarantee as it is about the longing. That means when you have hope in Heaven or Jesus, you are absolutely convinced and eagerly waiting for it. **Christian hope is a promise you can rest your weight on.**

A Messiah was promised from the beginning in the Garden of Eden when Adam and Eve failed to trust God. God promised to send a deliverer. Many great prophets and kings came and went, but none were the Messiah. The Israelites held out hope for a while but lost their confidence and assurance that he would come. Their grip weakened, and they let go of their hope. Yet, God remained faithful even as they gave up.

THE ANGEL'S HOPE

When the angels arrived at a little grassy hillside, they announced the rope hope was still there and as strong as ever.

> **"And the angel said to them, 'Fear not, for behold, I bring you good news of great joy that will be for all the people'" (Luke 2:10).**

The angels brought great hope. After this announcement, the shepherds traveled to Bethlehem to see it themselves. They shared the good news with others once they saw baby Jesus lying in a manger. Luke writes that all who heard the shepherd's story were astonished.

> **"And all who heard it were amazed at what the shepherds said to them"** (Luke 2:18).

But why? Wasn't a coming Messiah what they had been waiting for? It's one thing to want something wishfully. It's quite another to wait in anticipation, fully convinced that something is coming.

The Israelites hoped like we often hoped. I add a lot of hope to my cart. I hope Nathan gets into the college he wants, Brady wins his basketball tournament, and Zach and I stay healthy. These are important things, but I am talking about wishful thinking when I hope for these things. I'm still determining if they will happen. But when I hope in the things of God, I have a *tikvah* and *elpis* hope to work for me. It's not just wishful thinking. It's a promise I can count on.

The promises of God don't depend on you or me. They are a certainty. Jesus came to fulfill every promise and prophecy ever made about the coming Messiah. That's why he said in Matthew 5:17, **"Do not think that I have come to abolish the Law or the Prophets; I have not come to abolish them but to fulfill them."**

Lastly, the apostle Paul wrote these words in 2 Corinthians 1:20, **"For no matter how many promises God has made, they are 'Yes' in Christ. And so through him the 'Amen' is spoken by us to the glory of God."** God wants to convince you of everything he has promised. **When you let go of your rope hope, God never lets go of you.**

Anne Frank and her sister died in a concentration camp in February 1945. She never purchased toiletries or felt the sun on her face. But over thirty million copies of her book have been sold since. Her hope came true. Don't you wish you could have told her about it as she hid in that tiny alcove? *You will be a famous author!* How astonished she would have been.

Right now, like a little girl hidden in a wall, you are hiding in a world of sin and darkness. No one told Anne everything would work out. But we can encourage one another with God's promises. Your greatest wishes, deepest longings, and dreams of hope are all coming true through Jesus. You can count on it.

> "Where there's hope, there's life. It fills us with fresh courage and makes us strong again." — Anne Frank, *The Diary of a Young Girl*

UNBOX YOUR HOPE TODAY.

CHALLENGE DAY 2
HOPE: ADD TO CART

You add many things to your cart of life, looking for hope. Write down the top five things that bring you hope.

1 _____

2 _____

3 _____

4 _____

5 _____

While there are many ways that God gives hope to us, it's important to remember that the greatest hope comes from God. He should always be at the top of your list. Go to **www.redletterchallenge.com/adventverses** and read the ten Bible verses on hope. Write down and memorize one of the Bible verses as you unbox hope.

DAY 3 ✴

HOPE:

CHECKOUT

"IN HIS NAME THE NATIONS WILL PUT THEIR HOPE"
(MATTHEW 12:21).

HOPE IN THE WORLD

After you add something to your cart, it's time to enter the Checkout Stage. Every gift has a cost. Today, you will read about the enormous price tag Jesus paid to ensure you have the rope hope we added to your cart yesterday.

Ten years ago, the *United National General Assembly* proclaimed March 20 as the International Day of Happiness. Every year since then, *Gallup International* has released a *World Happiness Report* ranking each country by its self-proclaimed level of happiness. The report compares the average life satisfaction in different countries and discovers what features in the population explain these differences.

Here are some of the rankings from the 2023 report. The good ol' USA barely squeaked into the top 15, finishing 15th.

1. Finland	6. Sweden	11. Austria
2. Denmark	7. Norway	12. Australia
3. Iceland	8. Switzerland	13. Canada
4. Israel	9. Luxemburg	14. Ireland
5. Netherlands	10. New Zealand	15. United States

Here are the ten countries with the least happy ranking in the world.

128. Zambia	132. Botswana	135. Sierra Leone
129. Tanzania	133. Congo, Democratic Republic of	136. Lebanon
130. Comoros		137. Afghanistan
131. Malawi	134. Zimbabwe	

It's important to note that while some countries at the bottom were not experiencing any tragedy at the time of the survey, they still reported low happiness. Why were they sad even though their immediate circumstances were okay? Because happiness is not just about feeling safe and content in your present state. Happiness is also how confident you feel about your future.

Hope and happiness are very low in the Middle East and many African countries. People do not have access to healthcare if they become sick. Children's education often does not extend beyond elementary school. If famine or war comes, governments cannot protect their people and provide for them—an unsure future results in an unhappy present state.

Hope and happiness are intricately linked. In other words, people are hope-based creatures. **What you think about your future will drastically determine your present happiness.** As the *World Happiness Report* shows, hope isn't limited to the individual. Hope is a cultural necessity. Today, you will look at the wrong places people seek hope and where your true hope comes from.

THE HOPE OF THE UNITED STATES

We've examined hope in the world. Let's bring it closer to home and look at the hope of the United States. Professor Andrew Delbanco from Harvard wrote a small book called *The Real American Dream: A Meditation on Hope.* In its three chapters, Delbanco explains what he believes the United States has put its shared hope in as a nation.

1. In chapter one, the United States' hope was based on religion in its early days. Pilgrims left an oppressive regime and pursued religious freedom. Although it was not always perfect, under this hope, the nation was collectively united, even though there were many denominations and religious groups.

2. Hope shifted to the nation in the 19th century. In chapter two, Delbanco explains that there was high patriotism, and people were willing to die for their country. As "One Nation Under God," they had hope.

3. In chapter three, Delbanco demonstrates how the self is now the hope of American culture. People count on doing what makes them happy. Their hope to realize their full potential as a single person often becomes their primary pursuit. This hope must forge on to self-actualize and disregard everyone else's needs.[7]

Here's the problem: religion, politics, and self-hope are not cohesive. For a nation to be happy and hopeful, there needs to be something outside of ourselves that everyone can rally around and support. True hope in anything other than Jesus has a splintering effect.

All you have is a pile of toothpicks rather than one unified rope hope, and toothpicks snap quickly on their own.

THE HOPE OF ISRAEL

Did the people of the Bible have hope? Many prophets brought hope to Israel that a Messiah would come. The Gospel writer Matthew quoted a prophecy from Isaiah that claimed Jesus to be the promised Messiah.

> **Here is my servant whom I have chosen, the one I love, in whom I delight;**
> **I will put my Spirit on him, and he will proclaim justice to the nations.**
> **He will not quarrel or cry out; no one will hear his voice in the streets. A**
> **bruised reed he will not break, and a smoldering wick he will not snuff**
> **out, till he has brought justice through to victory. In his name the nations**
> **will put their hope. (Matthew 12:18-21)**

This prophecy reminded us that Jesus would not be the sole hope for Israel but for all nations. There is hope for you, too, included in all the nations. And while the hope of Jesus is offered to you, is it where you find your greatest hope?

THE HOPE OF OUR HEARTS

Yesterday, you read about the different things you add to your hope cart to find meaning and significance. Some people put their church and pastor as their hope. But the church is made up of broken people. Others put their nation in their hope cart. As long as their political party is in power, they have hope. But they panic when the tables turn. Finally, have you ever put your hope in yourself, believing you can only count on yourself?

Regardless of where you have searched for hope, a secure future is vital to having hop
But that kind of promise costs something which you cannot afford. It's a gift given to you.
Jesus offers it to anyone and everyone.

"VERY TRULY I TELL YOU, WHOEVER HEARS MY WORD AND BELIEVES HIM WHO SENT ME HAS ETERNAL LIFE AND WILL NOT BE JUDGED BUT HAS CROSSED OVER FROM DEATH TO LIFE" (JOHN 5:24).

The greatest hope has the greatest cost—far beyond what anyone could ever pay for themselves.

Jesus purchased a secure future for you so you can have hope in the present.

When you feel confident that you will be cared for, significant issues in your life become smaller. As you hit that "Buy it Now" button, don't take it for granted that the bill was paid in full at the cross. Thanks to God's payment, you have the promise of a resurrected new body, a place to live with God, and a reassurance that God is working it all out. Now that's a priceless gift I'm happy to receive!

UNBOX YOUR HOPE TODAY.

CHALLENGE DAY 3
HOPE: CHECKOUT

Knowing that God has secured your future, what are five promises you are looking forward to coming to completion? After you write them down, pray, thanking God for this future.

1 _____

2 _____

3 _____

4 _____

5 _____

DAY 4 ✶

HOPE:

IN TRANSIT

"JESUS LOOKED AT THEM AND SAID, 'WITH MAN THIS IS IMPOSSIBLE, BUT WITH GOD ALL THINGS ARE POSSIBLE'" (MATTHEW 19:26).

THE RETURN OF THE BOSS

The gift of hope has been paid for and is on its way. Now you are in full wait mode. Today, during the In Transit Stage, we will challenge you to practice disciplines that will prepare you for hope, like the famous explorer Ernest Shackleton and his men.

During one of his expeditions to the Antarctic, Sir Ernest Shackleton had to leave some of his men on Elephant Island. He intended to return for them and bring them back to England, but he was delayed.

By the time he returned for them, the sea had frozen, and he had no access to the island. He tried to reach them three times, but the ice prevented him. Finally, on his fourth try, 128 days later, he found a narrow channel.

To his surprise, he discovered the crew members waiting with supplies packed and ready to board. They were soon on their way back to England. He asked them how they knew to be prepared. They replied,

> "We did not know when you would return, but we were sure you would. So, every morning for all 128 days, the group leader rolled up his bag, packed his gear, and told us to get ready. He would always say the same thing, 'Get your things ready, boys. The boss may come today.'"[8]

Our boss, Jesus, can come anytime, too. We are all busy preparing for Christmas, but are we ready for God? Right now, Heaven is in transit. God's kingdom came in Jesus and is available now, but it is not in its fullness. God's kingdom still isn't as it should be. In the meantime, collectively, we are not waiting well.

If hope can make the difference between a happy and depressed person, then it feels like our nation has lost some of its hope. Social media allows us to present a facade that everything is alright, yet we all know that's not true. In a world where everyone has a platform, we have decided the last thing we want to show is our true selves. Is it only in modern times that people have felt this way?

THE HOPE OF A RICH MAN

Matthew writes of a wealthy person's quest for meaning. A rich young man came to Jesus asking how to get eternal life. What he was really after was hope.

> **Just then, a man came up to Jesus and asked, "Teacher, what good thing must I do to get eternal life?"**
>
> **"Why do you ask me about what is good?" Jesus replied. "There is only One who is good. If you want to enter life, keep the commandments."**

"Which ones?" he inquired.

Jesus replied, "'You shall not murder, you shall not commit adultery, you shall not steal, you shall not give false testimony, honor your father and mother,' and 'love your neighbor as yourself.'"

"All these I have kept," the young man said. "What do I still lack?"

Jesus answered, "If you want to be perfect, go, sell your possessions and give to the poor, and you will have treasure in heaven. Then come, follow me."

When the young man heard this, he went away sad because he had great wealth.

Then Jesus said to his disciples, "Truly I tell you, it is hard for someone who is rich to enter the kingdom of heaven. Again I tell you, it is easier for a camel to go through the eye of a needle than for someone who is rich to enter the kingdom of God" (Matthew 19:16-24).

The young man was looking for a way to earn money. Yesterday, we talked about the cost of hope. This young man not only wanted to see the bill, but he wanted to cover it himself. He thought he could earn a place in heaven if he did enough good.

But Jesus knew what was in the man's heart.

Even if the rich man had kept many of the outer commandments, he was guilty of breaking the first commandment, which is laid out in Exodus 20:3: **"You shall have no other gods before me."**

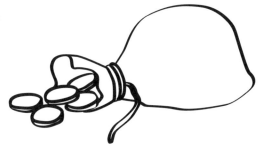

Jesus didn't want to prove to the young man that he was a bad person. He can only find hope in Jesus, not in following the rules. When he challenged him to sell all his possessions, it was to show the idolatry in his heart.

The young man was shocked. That bill was too high to pay, so he went away sad. He could not follow the Ten Commandments perfectly, after all. His rope hope was in his possessions, and he didn't want to pay if his current wealth was the cost of eternal life.

Unfortunately, he lost all he had when he died. His hope was in transit, but he gave up too quickly. Money and possessions were this man's idol; many of us still struggle with them today. Maybe your greatest hope is in your career, achievements, spouse, kids, or fill-in-the-blank. It won't hold up when you place your ultimate hope in anything other than Jesus. You will eventually lose everything in life because we all die. Everything, that is, but Jesus.

THE ALL-STAR VERSE

After the conversation with the young rich man, the disciples felt hopeless, too.

> **"When the disciples heard this, they were greatly astonished and asked, 'Who then can be saved?'" (Matthew 19:25).**

They knew they could not be perfect. They were right; they couldn't save themselves. Jesus confirmed their feelings and spoke right to their heart.

"JESUS LOOKED AT THEM AND SAID, 'WITH MAN THIS IS IMPOSSIBLE, BUT WITH GOD ALL THINGS ARE POSSIBLE'" (MATTHEW 19:26).

Some people have used part of this verse as inspiration to perform great acts of athleticism or to break a world record. When people take this verse and make it about them, they are missing the point. The verse has nothing to do with your ability to accomplish impossible things. It's all about God's ability to make the impossible possible for you. Despite all odds, salvation and eternity are secure for those who hope in Jesus.

Hope is in transit, but Jesus is already here. He is the assurance of a future and your solution to the false hopes you hold onto.

Shackleton's men hoped their boss would return for them. They waited 128 days. What if, on the 127th day, they decided it had been long enough, and they would figure something else out? They would have missed Shackleton's return. What if you don't wait long enough? What if you give up on God?

Here is the most fantastic news you will hear this holiday season. You are not on a deserted island waiting for your boss to return. He came! **You cannot miss the boat.** You are safely in transit, rescued by Jesus.

UNBOX YOUR HOPE TODAY.

CHALLENGE DAY 4
HOPE: IN TRANSIT

Deliver hope to someone who needs it this Christmas season. Just like Shackleton's men were ready daily, be prepared to give away hope to someone who needs it. Take a Ziploc bag and fill it with ways to bless someone. You can include warm socks, a gift card, an encouraging note, or basic hygiene necessities like a toothbrush, deodorant, or feminine products.

DAY 5

HOPE:

HANDLE
WITH CARE

"HE SAID TO THEM, 'THE SON OF MAN IS GOING TO BE DELIVERED INTO THE HANDS OF MEN. THEY WILL KILL HIM, AND AFTER THREE DAYS HE WILL RISE'" (MARK 9:31B).

THE GREATEST TOYMAKERS

When you purchase a gift online, you expect that gift to arrive in good order. Some boxes are filled with fragile or breakable items and have a sticker that says, "Handle with Care." Like boxes during the holiday season, we should also handle people with care. For some, the Advent season may be the loneliest, saddest, and darkest time of the year. It may be the season where a person feels less hope than at any other time of the year. One person who was filled with hopelessness may surprise you.

In October 2023, *Reuters* reported that Melissa and Doug, a toy company, was sold for $950 million. That deal was finalized at the beginning of 2024, making the company owners almost billionaires. It's impressive for a simple wooden toy company to report growth during the rise of technology, screens, and video games. Our boys had the Melissa and Doug wooden pizza set, and we had a lot of fun with it!

Melissa and Doug Bernstein, the founders and owners, live in a sprawling mansion in Westport, CT, where they raised their six children. We drove by their home in 2009 while visiting a church, and our host pointed it out. It was an idyllic family home.

That was the extent of what we knew about them until a CBS Sunday Morning interview with Melissa and Doug in March 2024.[9] The interview began with scenes inside their home and the couple playing with their six children. Despite the mansion behind them, they looked refreshingly normal. They didn't have fake tans, flashy diamonds, or fancy clothes. They seemed kind and down-to-earth.

But not everything was perfect. Melissa's memoir, *Lifelines*, was coming out that spring. In it, she wrote about the debilitating depression she suffered as a child. She called it existential depression. She shared the question that has been plaguing her entire life.

> **Why am I here? What is the meaning of life if we are all going to die ultimately?**

Writing allowed Melissa to overcome her fear, so she wrote three thousand verses like the one below.

> **I am fearful, oh so fearful; if you do not show me light, I will lose the will to live and choose to end this futile fight. — Melissa B., five-years-old.**

That's pretty deep for a five-year-old. Throughout her life, Melissa struggled with suicidal thoughts, eating disorders, and trying to control every single thing she could to feel better.

"I created a bottle of pills while a student at Duke University," Melissa Bernstein revealed in the interview. "I researched a cocktail of pills that would stop my heart, and carried it around for a year. I knew if the pain got too intense, it was there."

Career, success, and money didn't give her an answer to the meaning of life. Melissa now seeks to provide hope to others through her website and book. She reasoned that she would find meaning if she poured herself into helping others. Will it work?

Melissa is looking for hope. For me, this hope was only found by believing in Jesus and living out of that belief.

WAITING FOR HOPE

While it was apparent Melissa was looking for hope, it's not always that clear in others. Zach and I are now in our 40s, and I've noticed our peers dividing into different groups of hope.

When we were younger, it felt like most of us were on the same playing field. We were mostly bright-eyed and optimistic about the future and what it held. But through the hard knocks of life in our 20s and 30s, I've seen two groups emerge: the NOT GOTS and the GOTS.

GROUP #1: THE NOT GOTS

Some people have yet to get anything they hoped for. For many people, it wasn't their fault at all. Success can depend on the parents they were born into or the geographical location they were from. But other times, it could be a lost opportunity or poor choices on their part. Either way, for whatever reason, things didn't work out for them.

GROUP #2: THE GOTS

These people managed to get whatever it was they hoped for. It could be a job, a spouse, children, money, material possessions, good health, solid friendships, or fame. Like the NOT GOTS, the GOTS often got to where they are due to situations entirely out of their control. It matters where you were born, what period, who you know, and what your experiences are.

Would you call yourself a NOT GOT, a GOT, or somewhere in the middle? Maybe you can relate to one of these two camps. Regardless of where you fall, both groups still need help with hope. Let's start with those that haven't gotten what they hoped for.

It's common for the NOT GOTS to accuse life of not being fair. These people may find themselves blaming anything or anyone. They need to be handled with care.

The GOTS can be trickier, so I've divided them into three sub-groups. They got some things that they thought would bring happiness: great marriages, wonderful and healthy children, jobs they love, safe homes, cars, or friends who support them. But this group proves it's possible to get some things that you hope for and still struggle with hope.

Three different patterns can trend around middle age for the GOTS.

1 **Some keep searching for *it*.** They will struggle to find hope, especially if they have no relationship with God and don't see any value in faith. They relentlessly look for more of something because they are still not satisfied. *It's got to be out there somewhere; I have to find it*, they reason. People switch houses, spouses, and jobs to find the perfect one.

These people may find themselves exhausted from chasing. They need to be handled with care.

2 **Others transfer hope.** They might pour themselves into a cause, hoping to find their ultimate meaning as they become radically sold out for a mission. Rather than working alongside God in his work, the mission replaces God deep in their hearts. Obviously, some non-profit organizations, causes, and missions are great things to be a part of, and I strongly believe in them. However, the organization or mission in and of itself, even if it is good, cannot be the ultimate thing that gives you hope.

These people may find themselves disappointed. They need to be handled with care.

3 **Finally, some people give up hope**. Those in this group reason, *"Life is what it is, and it's nonsense to fantasize about more. Be realistic and give up your pie-in-the-sky dreams."* They sneer at any optimism and roll their eyes at the youth. They look down on others who cry at love stories, aspire to change the world, or believe in greatness because to need is to open yourself up to pain. It is better not to want anything than to be vulnerable.

These people are in jeopardy of becoming cynical. They need to be handled with care.

While in this place of transit, we need to care for the blaming, exhausted, disappointed, and cynical people and offer them hope because we are all those people at some point in our lives.

We've examined four reasons why people misplace hope. It's essential to handle people with care. But there's a fifth option, and it's the best one.

HOPE: THE BEST OPTION

The only way to find real hope and happiness is to place your hope in something outside this world. **You can set your hope in Jesus.**

All hope seemed lost when Jesus was in the grave for three days, but it shouldn't have been. Jesus told the disciples point-blank that this would happen. Read Mark's account below. Do you think Jesus was clear?

> **They went on from there and passed through Galilee. And he did not want anyone to know, for he was teaching his disciples, saying to them, 'The Son of Man is going to be delivered into the hands of men, and they will kill him. And when he is killed, after three days he will rise.' But they did not understand the saying and were afraid to ask him. (Mark 9:30-32)**

The disciples couldn't fathom that Jesus would rise again because death has always been the final blow. Yet, seven chapters later, an angel offered these words of hope to the women there to anoint the dead body of Jesus.

> **"'Don't be alarmed,' he said. 'You are looking for Jesus the Nazarene, who was crucified. He has risen! He is not here. See the place where they laid him'" (Mark 16:6).**

The angels handled the women with care. **Jesus is the hope this world is searching for.** Hope in Jesus saves you from the need to blame others, exhausting yourself in the rat race, experiencing crushing disappointments, and viewing the world with cynical eyes. Brokenness keeps many people from experiencing hope, so we must handle others with care.

UNBOX YOUR HOPE TODAY.

CHALLENGE DAY 5
HOPE: HANDLE WITH CARE

Melissa Bernstein wrote verses to combat her existential depression. She needed to be handled with care. I want to challenge you to do the same. But, rather than writing your verses, look up hope in your Bible and write down three verses that assure you of your salvation. If needed, you can revisit **www.redletterchallenge.com/adventverses**.

Which can you relate to the most?

☐ blaming   ☐ exhausted

☐ disappointed   ☐ cynical

DAY 6

HOPE:

DELIVERED

"WHERE IS THE ONE WHO HAS BEEN BORN KING OF THE JEWS? WE SAW HIS STAR WHEN IT ROSE AND HAVE COME TO WORSHIP HIM" (MATTHEW 2:2B).

SETTING UP THE NATIVITY

As you examine the hope God gives you, I want to take you back to a significant group of characters in the Christmas story and the hopeful message behind them.

Our Willow Tree nativity is a staple Christmas decoration for our family. It has traveled with us to apartments in St. Louis, our home in Florida, and now our current home in Nebraska. After twenty Christmases, it's a little worse for wear. One of our three wise men had his head glued back on after being dropped by Nathan. Our youngest son, Brady, decorated a sheep's white coat with a green magic marker. Scrapes and all, we will display our nativity every Christmas because it tells the beautiful story of royalty at Jesus's birth. It always made me feel warm and fuzzy to set out the three kings on the left with the shepherds on the right. Make room for everyone around the manger of Baby Jesus!

So, you can see my surprise when I learned that the wise men, also called the Magi, were not kings. The crowns on their heads and colored robes always made me assume they were esteemed royalty, traveling like Prince Ali from the movie Aladdin and laying their gifts at the feet of Jesus. I wondered, *"If they aren't royalty, what else am I missing about the wise men?"*

As I investigated who these wise men were, I found that many of my assumptions about them could be wrong.

DEBUNKING MAGI MYTHS

Let's start with the famous Christmas hymn *We Three Kings*.

Just singing the first line, *"We three kings of the Orient are,"* might be enough to allow you to sing the song from memory. But even in the first line, there are already two potential myths.

MYTH 1: THREE?

One potential error is that we assume that there were three of these characters. The Bible never says. We know it was more than one since they were Magi, which is plural. Maybe it is assumed three because three gifts were given to Jesus: gold, frankincense, and myrrh. But maybe there were only two Magi, and they were generous. Or maybe there were seven or ten or forty!

MYTH 2: KINGS?

This hymn also makes you think these three Magi were kings. But the Magi were not kings. In the Bible, the Magi are members of a Persian priestly class, perhaps astrologers or interpreters of celestial signs. A reference to the Magi in the Old Testament that the readers of Matthew's Gospel would have known was the story from Daniel 2:1-13. King Nebuchadnezzar brought the Magi to interpret one of his dreams in this narrative. When they could not interpret it, the king ordered that the Magi would be executed and put to death. Thankfully, Daniel stepped in, interpreted the king's dream, and saved the lives of these Magi. When you look into the story, you see that the Magi were not kings. They were servants of the king. And servants that could be disposed of just like that. (Gulp!)

MYTH #3: STABLE?

In many retellings of the story of Jesus's birth, the Magi are right there at the stable, seeing baby Jesus. However, Luke's gospel only mentions shepherds and angels there. If the Magi were from Persia, it would have been more than a 1200-mile journey. It's far more likely that Jesus was around a year old and nowhere near the stable when the Magi arrived.

MYTH #4: WISE?

Another name for the Magi is wise men. But were they even wise? The story written in the Book of Daniel depicts them as unwise, powerless, and disposable servants. Even in the story from Matthew 2, they could have been wiser than we give them credit for. When they saw the star, they went to the palace and asked for directions. Then, upon receiving direction, God dropped a star blatantly over the house of Jesus that they couldn't miss it. Matthew's narrative presents the Magi as ignorant compared to Herod, the chief priests, and even the readers. The Magi seem to know less about what is going on than anyone else.

So, are you ready to throw out your three Magi figurines yet? Before they go in the trash, keep reading. Let me tell you who they are and why a more proper understanding makes the Christmas story even better.

THE DEEPER CHRISTMAS MESSAGE

The Magi symbolize the hope that the birth of Jesus delivered. As you read about the Magi's encounter with King Herod and the religious leaders of Israel, you see a stark contrast between worldly wisdom and divine revelation. While Herod and the chief priests had all the knowledge of Scripture in their hands, they lacked the humility and faith to recognize that the promises were finally coming true right in their backyards.

In contrast, despite their ignorance of Jewish customs and traditions, the Magi followed a tiny twinkle of a promise and traveled far from their home. They were among the first to bow down before the promised Messiah. The Magi weren't just delivering gifts; they were delivering hope for all of us who have been counted as out. They may have asked simple questions, but the Magi had great faith.

> **"Where is the one who has been born king of the Jews?
> We saw his star when it rose and have come to worship him"**
> **(Matthew 2:2b).**

It's time for us to reevaluate our assumptions about who God's hope is actually for. Why would God choose such unlikely messengers like the Magi, individuals who neither worshiped him nor held positions of power in their country? The answer lies in the profound message of hope woven throughout the Christmas story.

If we have a story of God coming to the wise and the intelligent, then it goes against everything our God says he is for. Jesus says in Matthew 11:25,

> **"I praise you, Father, Lord of heaven and earth, because you have hidden these things from the wise and learned, and revealed them to little children."**

When we understand the inclusion of the Magi in this story, we begin to understand what Christmas is all about. As you gather around your nativity sets this Christmas, I hope you have a newfound connection with those three figurines. I sure do. These men show me that God uses people I would never pick out to accomplish his tasks. God manifests himself to the ignorant, the fools, those on the B-team, those far away, and those who have been disposed of or even laughed at and misunderstood.

God's plan of salvation transcends religious norms and expectations and includes all people, regardless of their status or background.

Your guiding star of hope may be small, but it twinkles brightly. Despite your bumps, scrapes, and magic marker stains, receive the hope of Jesus today.

UNBOX YOUR HOPE TODAY.

CHALLENGE DAY 6
HOPE: DELIVERED

Move your Magi. If you display a nativity at home, move your wise men far from it. As each day passes, move them closer and closer to it. This activity will build hope by reminding you that Jesus is coming, even for those far away.

Read about the Magi from Matthew 2:1-12.

OPTIONAL CHALLENGE

If you don't have a nativity set, consider purchasing one this year and practicing this tradition. If you already have one, consider giving one away to someone else.

DAY 7

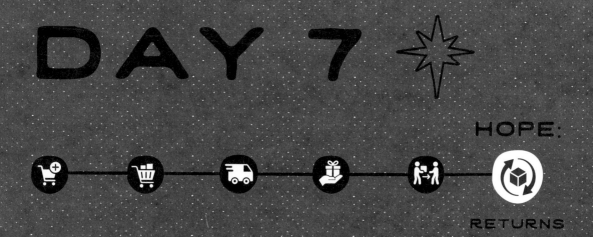

HOPE:

RETURNS

"JESUS ANSWERED, 'EVERYONE WHO DRINKS THIS WATER WILL BE THIRSTY AGAIN, BUT WHOEVER DRINKS THE WATER I GIVE THEM WILL NEVER THIRST.'" (JOHN 4:13-14A).

HOPE IN THE DARKNESS

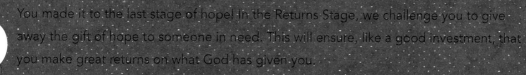

You made it to the last stage of hope! In the Returns Stage, we challenge you to give away the gift of hope to someone in need. This will ensure, like a good investment, that you make great returns on what God has given you.

Gloria Umanah is a first-generation Nigerian-American born in Atlanta, GA. As a little girl, she experienced an overwhelming hopelessness that no child should experience. She lived below the poverty line, moving to over ten different motel rooms with her immigrant mother and four sisters after being abandoned by her father.

Fed up with what life was offering her, sixteen-year-old Gloria planned to take her own life at a church retreat. As she stood up to leave, feeling lonelier than she had ever felt in her entire life, she scanned the crowded room, looking for the nearest exit. Finding it and proceeding to walk out, as her hand gripped the handle and pushed through the heavy door, the worship leader called out a message of hope from the stage. The musician declared that someone in the room was contemplating suicide. He begged for this person to come forward instead and receive prayer.

Hope had found Gloria. She made a 180-degree turn that night, literally and in her heart. God used that moment to call her out of the darkness and into his glorious light.

HOPE IN SUPERHEROES AND MONSTERS

The entertainment world always wants to make returns on its investment in making movies. So, they use false hope to capture people's interests. Here are some examples,

1 In 2017, *The Shape of Water* received 263 nominations and 91 wins at award shows from critics.[10] The movie was about a woman who fell in love with a half-human, half-sea creature. Ultimately, she turned into a half-sea creature herself and lived forever underwater. The director won a Golden Globe for Best Director, and the movie won two Academy Awards. People hope for true love outside this world.

2 Marvel is known for famous superheroes such as Spider-man, Wolverine, Iron Man, Captain America, Thor, Hulk, Daredevil, Dr. Strange, Black Panther, Avengers, X-Men, Fantastic Four, and Guardians of the Galaxy, to name a few. An article published for *Harvard Business Review* detailed the impact of these movies. The last 22 films have grossed over $17 billion—more than any other movie franchise.[11] The films average an 84% approval rating on Rotten Tomatoes and have received 64 nominations and awards per movie. People hope that the superhero can save the world.

3 One of the best-selling books ever written, J.R.R. Tolkien's *Lord of the Rings*, is set in an imaginary world called Middle Earth. It has sold 150 million copies. People hope that another world exists outside our own where supernatural beings exist.

Why do people desire to watch or read about a deep physical, spiritual, and emotional connection with the supernatural if there is no such thing? These readers and critics are brilliant, grown, logical adults who read and watch hundreds of books and movies annually. Why would a fictional sea monster, superheroes, and hobbits in a pretend world be so intriguing? Heaven is real because the supernatural does exist, and we are supposed to live forever.

Your deepest longings are evidence of the truth.

WATER THAT SATISFIES

One day, Jesus ran into a Samaritan woman who placed all her hope in human relationships. Having had multiple relationships, she was an outcast in her village. So, the Samaritan woman went alone to the well at noon to avoid the gossip. Scholars wonder, was the woman responsible for all her failed relationships, or was she the innocent victim of men using her? While we may not know for sure, Jesus was sure ready to meet her and give her the hope she'd always wanted.

In John 4, you can read Jesus's longest recorded one-on-one conversation. It is with this woman at the well. As they talked, she saw that this was a divine encounter. He understood her situation like no one had ever done before. She was going there to get some drinking water, but Jesus had something supernatural for her instead.

> **"Jesus answered, 'Everyone who drinks this water will be thirsty again, but whoever drinks the water I give them will never thirst. Indeed, the water I give them will become in them a spring of water welling up to eternal life'" (John 4:13-14).**

There's that mention of eternal life again. Living forever and being eternally satisfied and loved are some of the deepest hopes of our souls. This woman not only received the gift of Jesus, but then she went on to share who Jesus was and deliver hope to her town.

And look at how hope multiplied throughout Samaria.

"MANY OF THE SAMARITANS FROM THAT TOWN BELIEVED IN HIM BECAUSE OF THE WOMAN'S TESTIMONY" (JOHN 4:39A).

The woman who was the talk of the town became quite the talker in the town.

The beautiful message of the Christmas season is that your deepest longings will find you in Jesus. He came in human flesh and humility to fulfill your deepest longing.

Your hope found you!

Gloria received hope on her darkest night but realized it was not meant just for her. Just like the Samaritan woman, Gloria shared what Jesus had done for her and helped others receive hope. Today, Gloria leads a project called *The Hope Booth*, creating returns on the hope she was given. *The Hope Booth* is a project dedicated to renovating old telephone booths into places where people can get a hope-filled interactive and immersive experience. Her project is giving hope to thousands every day.

Gloria's example is what we hope happens in your life with the hope you unbox. After unboxing, you have the option to create returns on that gift. Just like these two women, you can give the hope of Jesus away to others.

UNBOX YOUR HOPE TODAY.

[To hear the rest of Gloria's story and more information about Hope Booth, you can listen to her interview, *Gloria Umanah: Tackling Suicide, Christian Mental Health, & Hope for America*, on *The Red Letter Disciple Podcast*.][12]

CHALLENGE DAY 7
HOPE: RETURNS

Give hope to someone today. Who do you know who needs hope? Whether through an encouraging word, an act of service, or a financial gift, reach out to someone who needs hope and provide hope for that person today.

DAYS
8-13

✦

OF ADVENT

"I HAVE TOLD YOU THESE THINGS, SO
THAT IN ME YOU MAY HAVE PEACE."

JOHN 16:33A

WEEK OF

PEACE

DAY 8

PEACE:

**ADD
TO CART**

"PEACE I LEAVE WITH YOU; MY PEACE I GIVE YOU. I DO NOT GIVE
TO YOU AS THE WORLD GIVES. DO NOT LET YOUR HEARTS BE
TROUBLED AND DO NOT BE AFRAID" (JOHN 14:27).

HOW THE WORLD GIVES PEACE

Like with hope, you can add many peaceful things to the cart, but not everything is the best. Today, we begin unboxing peace by examining how people try to achieve peace in our world. One example is from a book by Roy T. Bennett.

In 2016, Bennett wrote *The Light in the Heart* to help people live peacefully. In the book, he encouraged people to think positively and focus on the good. He wrote, "Learning to distance yourself from all the negativity is one of the greatest lessons to achieve inner peace."

According to Bennett, the most effective way to keep the peace was to avoid any place where conflict exists. Many self-described peacemakers have embraced this philosophy. "Good vibes only!" is a famous slogan today that follows this thought.

In today's reading, I want to discuss three false definitions of peace and how Jesus defines peace differently. That's the peace you wish to add to your cart.

1 The first understanding of peace is avoiding all conflict and negativity. This is what Bennett was aiming at. For him, to keep peace, you should avoid all conflict.

2 A second understanding of peace is one-sided domination over another. You keep peace by obtaining complete power and authority over another. For example, the Romans named the period between 27 BCE and 180 CE "Pax Romana," which means Roman Peace. For the Romans, peace was when they overtook others and ruled with an iron fist. But their idea of peace was brutal, forced, and deadly to the opposition.

3 Lastly, many define peace as having perfect behavior. The best way to achieve peace is to live without making any mistakes. The more rules, the better. Peace means perfect performance for them. Peace comes through achievement and adherence to a code.

None of these were how Jesus brought peace.

I DO NOT GIVE AS THE WORLD GIVES

In our Bible verse for today, you see Jesus offering a different kind of peace.

"PEACE I LEAVE WITH YOU; MY PEACE I GIVE YOU. I DO NOT GIVE TO YOU AS THE WORLD GIVES. DO NOT LET YOUR HEARTS BE TROUBLED AND DO NOT BE AFRAID" (JOHN 14:27).

So, what peace did Jesus bring? Avoiding conflict, dominating others, or demanding perfect performance out of others is not how Jesus brought peace. Perfect performance was necessary, but not by you. Jesus's perfect life fulfilled what we could not. If we defined Jesus's peace in these terms, we would have examples of him steering clear of people who disagreed with him, dominating others, or being a strict tyrant about rules and regulations. He would only choose successful people and winners. But you won't see Jesus doing any of these things.

Jesus walked right into conflict. From a young age, Jesus put himself in situations with opposing sides. When he was only twelve, he went to the synagogue and asked the church leaders difficult questions. His first miracle involved a party and alcohol. Jesus had many meals with people who were outcasts and looked down upon. Jesus stood up against Jewish groups like the Sadducees and Pharisees when they tried to trap him. Jesus headed to Jerusalem, the hot seat of conflict between the Roman and Jewish people.

Jesus's love was for everyone. Jesus brought peace to earth by seeking the right relationships with all people, including his enemies. If this is true, then it means something astounding.

PEACEMAKING WILL NOT ALWAYS BE PEACEFUL.

Unlike Bennett, who advised people to run in the other direction as soon as they saw any disputes, Jesus headed toward conflict areas to make peace.

A peacemaker is someone who doesn't just go where there is conflict but someone who brings opposing sides together.

That kind of action is not going to be clean and tidy. To stand in the middle means you not only have to witness some ugly behavior. You might even find yourself caught in the crossfire.

Peacemaking will not always be peaceful.

After Peter refused to let Jesus wash his feet, Jesus responded with the verse for today. Peter didn't understand that Jesus was making peace by serving. Immediately afterward, John tells us that Jesus began predicting his death, which was the ultimate act of peacemaking between God and his people. But would the disciples see it that way?

Not at all! They were upset and confused. Bringing peace means things are going to get messy quickly.

THE NEED FOR PEACE

On the inside, the opposite of peace is anxiety. According to *Forbes*, in 2023, anxiety disorders are now affecting 19.1% of adults, nearly 40 million in our nation. In addition, almost 50% of those 18-24 years of age experience depressive disorder or anxiety symptoms. Finally, half of our fifty states have 50% of people who feel nervous, anxious, or on edge at least several days a week.[13] None of that is good.

On the outside, the opposite of peace is war. I read an article suggesting that 92% of recorded history includes war and national violence stories. In the last 3400 years, only

268 years have gone by without war. That statistic is staggering! A glance at national and international news would indicate this is true. The world is in constant conflict.

Is all this outer conflict coming from our inner angst? The root word for anxiety in Greek is *merizo* which means to divide. Anxiety causes division. So, the more anxiety we have on the inside, the more division we experience on the outside.

There's so much happening in our lives and so much expected of us that something has to give. It's no wonder we have anxiety. If we are going to be a part of Jesus's peacemaking efforts, we should expect conflict, difficulty, and pain.

Being a peacemaker means we may get caught in the crossfire between two opposing sides. Jesus has made peace with us, so we would make peace with others. As we unbox the gift of peace, the ultimate goal is that you will not only receive his peace but also give it away to others. But what I find most comforting about Jesus's words to us is that we are not doing this alone.

The peace you bring in the middle of conflict is not by your strength but by the peace of Jesus. When you have to deal with friends who disagree with you, or a disrespectful child, or confront a spouse, or speak up in a meeting for something you believe is right, you don't have to have to be afraid. God will give you peace that differs from anything the world says.

God's peace is better than any peace this world can offer. It's a peace you can carry in your heart and will stand the test of time.

UNBOX YOUR PEACE TODAY.

CHALLENGE DAY 8
PEACE: ADD TO CART

Write down the top five things that bring you peace.

1. Spend time w/ friend & family
2. Attend Church
3. Attend Bible Study
4. Spend time with God
5. Time in Bed.   Video of ocean waves

While there are many ways that God gives peace to you, it's important to remember that true peace comes from God. He should always be at the top of the list. Go to **www.redletterchallenge.com/adventverses** and read the ten Bible verses on peace. Write down and memorize one of the Bible verses as you unbox peace.

DAY 9

PEACE:

CHECKOUT

"IF YOU, EVEN YOU, HAD ONLY KNOWN ON THIS DAY WHAT WOULD BRING YOU PEACE—BUT NOW IT IS HIDDEN FROM YOUR EYES" (LUKE 19:42).

BUSTED BULBS, BUSTED HOPES

My family had awesome Christmas traditions that I remember growing up, but hanging Christmas lights wasn't one of them. So, when I had my kids, I was determined that we would hang Christmas lights. The first year my wife and our two sons moved to Florida, I had no excuses. It was time! The only extra cost to my endeavor was $50 for the string lights. That was a small price for a house that would light up the neighborhood.

After hours of blood, sweat, and maybe even a tear or two, six strings of lights stretched across the front of the house. I had done it. When night fell, it was time for the grand reveal. My wife and two kids counted down, Griswold-style, and BANG! All the lights turned on!

It was a modest display of simple string lights on our gutters, but to me, it looked amazing. I knew all the hard work that had gone into it, and I was so proud. That's when everything changed.

Ten seconds into our oohs and aahs, it went pitch black. I was so confused. What happened?! Allison said we probably blew a fuse, so I went to the store, brought home a few fuses, and tried again. Everyone ran back outside for my second reveal. Drumroll, please! I plugged them in, and ten seconds later, the fuse blew. After multiple trips to the store and receipts piling up on the kitchen counter, we still had no shining lights.

A neighbor suggested I needed the correct GFCI box or something like that, so I brought out an electrician. That was another bill to pay. My plan to hang six simple string lights on an afternoon and not spend a ton was backfiring. Plus, I was starting to get jealous. When I compared my lights to other homes on my street with dozens of perfectly hung and lit strings, they made my feeble attempts even more pitiful. I began wondering what was wrong with me. Why was I so bad at this?

We were now out $400 for six little strings of lights that turned on only half the time. And even when they turned on, they wouldn't last the whole night before blowing a fuse again. What started as a minor expense slowly ate away at our Christmas budget. The cost was too high, and I was mad.

THE GRAND DISPLAY

The Zehnder home never got its grand display that year. My wife and sons took over in the coming years, and now we have a beautifully lit home every year. While I still admire the Christmas lights every evening as I pull into the garage, I can't help but carry a little grudge about the whole thing. I couldn't get those lights to work and wasted so much time and money trying to do so.

As you gaze upon Christmas lights this year, remember that you are looking at someone's final scene. You see the end result but miss the hard work and time it took.

When Christmas lights work correctly, they are a peaceful sight. They bring hope that even in darkness, light can still shine through. In Nebraska, where I now live, the sun sets before 5 p.m. in December, and we don't get too much sun. The lights can distract us from the otherwise pretty gloomy darkness.

As humans, we like looking at the final scenes. You may plan to drive around with your family this holiday and look at the lights. It's a fun tradition! But every final scene comes with a cost.

FAKE CHRISTMAS SCENE

Speaking of scenes, most of us love the nativity scene, where baby Jesus is lying in a manger, all cute and snuggly. We'll sing about it like this:

The cattle are lowing
The poor baby wakes
But little Lord Jesus
No crying He makes

So, the cows are just gently mooing, and the baby awakes and is not crying? When has a baby ever woken up and not cried? Nothing is cute about how the world's Savior was brought into this life. The unrealistic Hallmark-like scene might make you feel good, but it's likely not accurate and it came at a very high cost. There was a far greater rescue story behind this whole thing than a non-crying baby and a mooing cow.

Herod was about to issue a decree to kill every baby boy under the age of two.

The risk of being born to a mother out of wedlock was disastrous for a family's reputation.

Traveling away from your home in the last month of your pregnancy was dangerous to the mother and was a risk for the baby.

Mary and Joseph were poor, young, and inexperienced parents. Putting the fate of the world in their hands was a massive risk.

The cost of sending Jesus to Bethlehem was incredibly high.

THE REAL CHRISTMAS COST

Christmas morning was God's plan to bring everlasting peace to the world. And yet, it too was just a scene amid the grand story. Despite this significant risk and high cost, Jesus would survive this scene. He grew in wisdom, stature, and favor. Jesus opened blind eyes. He caused the lame to walk, the deaf to hear, and the mute to speak. He taught with authority unlike any who had ever gone before him. He was respected and followed by many. Riding in on a donkey, the crowd celebrated him as the king. But then Jesus said,

"IF YOU, EVEN YOU, HAD ONLY KNOWN ON THIS DAY WHAT WOULD BRING YOU PEACE—BUT NOW IT IS HIDDEN FROM YOUR EYES" (LUKE 19:42).

Jesus could see what the crowd couldn't that day. He knew that to get to the final scene of ultimate peace, it would require another scene—a scene of complete brutality and the death of his body on the cross. The crowd was so focused on what was before them that they missed out on God's bigger plan to bring peace to the world.

Jesus went from the scene of lying in a wooden box at his birth to stretching his hands on a wooden cross, dying for sins he never committed. This scene wasn't pretty either. There weren't any lights, sparkling snow, or smiling inflatable animals. It was a dirty, bloody mess. People averted their eyes and ran in the opposite direction. The cost of this scene was more incredible than anything you can ever imagine. It was a cost only one could pay, and that was Jesus.

To reach the final scene, where you and I live peacefully with God forever, someone had to pay the cost. Jesus paid that cost in full. In the end, when he rose from the dead, there were no false alarms, fuses failing, or burnt bulbs. Instead, there was a light that broke through the darkness.

"THE LIGHT SHINES IN THE DARKNESS, AND THE DARKNESS HAS NOT OVERCOME IT" (JOHN 1:5).

Jesus, the pure light of the world, was shining bright for all to see again. **Jesus paid for peace in full.**

UNBOX YOUR PEACE TODAY.

CHALLENGE DAY 9
PEACE: CHECKOUT

What was the cost for Jesus to bring peace? Your response to Jesus's sacrifice is to shine that peace into the world. Spend some time today and go out and look at some Christmas lights. As you do, remind yourself and those you are with that Jesus is the light of this world.

OPTIONAL CHALLENGE

If you haven't already, put some lights out this year. Perhaps it's something outside, a fireplace, or a candle inside. Shining lights in the darkness is not only a great reminder of what Jesus has done for us, but it's also a reminder of how he has called us to be lights in this world today.

DAY 10

PEACE:

IN TRANSIT

"COME TO ME, ALL YOU WHO ARE WEARY AND BURDENED, AND I WILL GIVE YOU REST" (MATTHEW 11:28).

MAXED OUT

Despite boasting a nation with a surging economy, comfortable homes, stocked pantry shelves, shiny new inventions, and unsurpassed communication technology, the USA consistently ranks among the world's top 10 most stressed nations. The Advent season is one of, if not the most stressful.

It's important to note first and foremost that the Bible never promises that you won't have stress, even if you believe in and follow Jesus. Pursuing an entirely problem-free life is not a godly pursuit, nor is it even a good goal. However, God promises us that we can have peace in the middle of difficulty.

While it's natural to feel some anxiety, it's important to remember that you don't have to be as stressed as you are. You have the power to cut unnecessary trouble out of your life. But where would you begin? Let's explore some strategies together.

THE STRESS TRIFECTA

One helpful exercise is to identify where your stress is coming from. While many things may cause you stress, much of it can be boiled down to three primary culprits: relationships, time, and money.

RELATIONSHIPS: People, especially during Advent, pull us in many different directions. To make others happy, many, including myself, find it easy to say "yes" to everybody else's requests. So, here's what you need to tell yourself:

I CANNOT BE EVERYTHING FOR EVERYBODY.

Only God can satisfy someone's deepest needs and longings. So, this may sound harsh initially, but you need to decide ahead of time who gets to be in a relationship with you and at what level. This pre-decision will help eliminate so much unnecessary stress. Modern-day research shows a person can only maintain 5-10 deep relationships. Who are those people for you?

Indeed, we don't need to be rude to others who may not fall into that category, but even Jesus prioritized relationships. He had a group of 72 dedicated followers with whom he spent much time. But, his most commonly known group was the twelve disciples. They got more access than the 72. Of the twelve, he had a group of three: Peter, James, and John. And, of course, he would often get away and spend time with his clear #1, God the Father.

TIME: If your life is like mine, then there is no busier season filled with more options of things to do than the Advent season. Between all of the people who need my time to uphold the many traditions that come alongside the season, it's too much. By the time I get to Christmas Eve, I'm exhausted. This sprint to get through the season reminds me that something isn't right. So, just like we had a declaration with relationships, we have one with time. Say this to yourself:

I CANNOT DO EVERYTHING I WANT TO DO.

Again, similar to relationships, you need to decide what you will do with your time ahead of time. If you don't, other people's priorities will quickly become yours. I've noticed that nobody genuinely asks me to care for my needs or priorities. The emails, texts, messages, or phone calls I receive are to help take care of other people's issues. As a follower of Jesus, I want to help others, but I can only be the best help if I'm healthy.

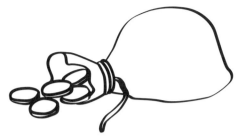

MONEY: Despite economic prosperity like never before, money is still the number one stressor in America. It's the number one reason for fighting in marriages and, sadly, the number one cause of divorce as well. So, even with great collective financial blessing, we need another declaration. Say this to yourself:

I CANNOT BUY EVERYTHING THAT I WANT TO BUY.

Like with relationships and time, we have a decision to make with finances. In the financial world, they have a word for it. Budget. A budget helps you to decide ahead of time what and how you will spend your money. Along these lines, Pastor Andy Stanley once said, "You should be a-knowin' where your money is a-goin'."

As I mentioned on Day One, the Christmas season in America is now a trillion-dollar industry. How we haphazardly spend our money in December not only creeps over into other parts of the year but also causes undue stress on our finances.

I must admit that I have picked these three culprits because these are not things you can eliminate in your life. You have to learn how to live with them. Just because we can't eliminate them doesn't mean we can't reduce our stress. But how?

The answer, just like *Jeopardy*, starts with a question.

THE BEST QUESTION EVER

I first learned this question from Andy Stanley's book entitled *The Best Question Ever*. I was skeptical. The question is only three words. I wondered, *"Will it make a difference in my life?"* After practicing this question for eight years, the answer is a resounding "Yes"! I'll admit that mastering this question takes work—hard work. But if you can get it right or even begin making progress, you can eliminate up to half of your unnecessary stress.

So, here's the stress-reducing question:

Asking this question before every problematic, complicated, or upcoming decision is a game-changer. Operating in wisdom is the key to eliminating half of your stress in life.

The great news is that if you need help making wise decisions, you have a God who loves giving you good gifts. Not only is he delivering gifts of hope, peace, joy, and love for you to unbox, but he's also ready for you to unbox his wisdom at any time.

"If any of you lacks wisdom, you should ask God, who gives generously to all without finding fault, and it will be given to you." James 1:5

If you need more wisdom, rest assured, God will generously provide it to you. His wisdom is not limited, but abundant, ready to support you in every decision you make.

The question may be simple to memorize, but it takes work to practice. The best way to progress with this question is to put it into practice. If you ask this question before making decisions, I guarantee you will eliminate unnecessary stress.

But because we are not living in a perfect world and are still awaiting Jesus's return, we will never have a stress-free life. So, what do we do?

TIME FOR A YOKE

One of the most popular phrases people think is a Bible verse is that "God will never give you more than you can handle." But that's not in the Bible. What is true is that God will never give you more than he can handle.

When stress comes your way, here is Jesus's invitation to you from Matthew 11:28-30.

> **"Come to me, all you who are weary and burdened, and I will give you rest. Take my yoke upon you and learn from me, for I am gentle and humble in heart, and you will find rest for your souls. For my yoke is easy and my burden is light."**

At first, this sounds counterintuitive. In stress reduction, we typically try to get things removed from us, not put on us. And yet, Jesus's invitation requires us to put on something. He asks us to put on his yoke.

What is a yoke? No, I'm not talking about the yellow part of the center of the egg. A yoke is a farming tool or instrument that binds two animals together to allow them to work more effectively. God is not interested in removing hard work from us. Instead, he invites us into a relationship where we never need to experience this world without him. We can walk and work together with him. We are yoked with him.

When two animals are yoked together, they move in the same direction and accomplish more. Jesus keeps us on the path when we are yoked together and walking and working with him. So, anytime something feels hard, it's vital to remember we are walking in unison with the one who knows what it's like to have the heaviest load of the world on his shoulders and come out victorious.

So, you must ask yourself: *"Is it wise for you to carry all this stress by yourself?"* Or *"Is it wise to give it to Jesus?"*

You are not meant to carry all of the hard stuff of this world alone. You have a God who came down to live as one of us. He knows what it's like to live in this world. He knows what managing relationships, prioritizing time, and stewarding resources are like. In any difficulty you may experience, he invites you not to walk alone but to be yoked together with him. So, while you can't eliminate all the stress of this world, the invitation of the Advent season is that Jesus will do anything to ensure you are yoked with him.

You can have his peace no matter what comes your way!

UNBOX YOUR PEACE TODAY.

CHALLENGE DAY 10
PEACE: IN TRANSIT

Cut unnecessary stress. Begin by praying to God and asking for wisdom. Then, ask, *"Is it wise?"* about some decisions you've made in relationships, time, and money this Advent season. Next, decide wisely to cut one unnecessary stressor in each of the three culprits: relationships, time, and money.

DAY 11

PEACE:

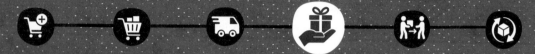

HANDLE
WITH CARE

"I HAVE TOLD YOU THESE THINGS, SO THAT IN ME YOU MAY HAVE PEACE. IN THIS WORLD YOU WILL HAVE TROUBLE. BUT TAKE HEART! I HAVE OVERCOME THE WORLD" (JOHN 16:33).

THE NOT-SO-PERFECT FAMILY

One year, I received a Christmas card from a large church in my area. At first glance, it looked like a department store ad rather than a church mailing. In the picture, the pastor's family laughed, posing perfectly, and dressed to coordinate a scenic background. They looked flawless.

I don't know this family, but I'm sure they are wonderful people. I hadn't been to their church, so I am not here to make judgments on the family or the church. However, I had mixed reactions when I received the card because all I knew about it was the image, which was too squeaky clean.

The card made me think that the church was a place for perfect families—or a place to become perfect. The problem is that I knew my family was nothing like that, and therefore, I couldn't help but feel like we wouldn't belong there. I was just about to throw away the mailer when I glanced down and saw our Christmas card for that year sitting on the counter. It looked eerily similar, and my stomach dropped.

Our photo was taken at sundown, so golden rays shone through the fall leaves behind us. My wife was smiling sweetly, her hair curled and lipstick applied. She looked beautiful. Our boys were wearing matching sweaters and bookending in perfect symmetry. I stood in the center of the frame, the strong and sturdy rock of the family. Our dog Ziggy was sitting at my feet, his pink tongue out as if he were smiling for the shot.

Maybe we would be welcomed into that "perfect family church" after all. And that was a problem because we are not, and have never been, perfect.

BEHIND CLOSED DOORS

I could spend a lot of time telling you how not perfect that picture is: how my dog pooped right in the place we were supposed to sit or that the boys hated their itchy sweaters. I could tell you that Allison and I weren't speaking because I had gotten home later than promised, and she had no help. On top of that, the freezing 22-degree wind was cutting through our already icy family photo like razer knives.

But you have been there. You get it. Pictures don't always paint the truth. Perfection is never what it seems, and that day, the sweet photographer handled our family with care.

That got me thinking: maybe we don't do this in family photos. Maybe without knowing it, we can project "the perfect Christian." We show up to volunteer, give to worthy causes, post Bible verses, and display Christian messages around our homes.

However, hidden underneath these "perfect Christian" actions are people who are not perfect. Behind closed doors, painful scenes unfold. Maybe one or two of these hit closer to home for you this Advent season:

* A mother and daughter are refusing to talk.

* A husband is weeping because it's the first Christmas without his wife.

* A daughter's drug problem has decimated the family.

* A dad's drinking makes him violent.

* A mom cries because her son has been deployed just before Christmas.

* A teenage son lost his virginity and sits in suffering and shame.

* A hopeless marriage is unraveling.

* A job loss prevents normal fun activities.

No matter what the Christmas card looks like, no perfect families are on this side of Heaven. As you read on Day 9, the scene from the original Christmas family was also not so perfect either. It was downright messy. Consider the following:

* Baby Jesus came from a family tree that included a prostitute, a murderer, and wicked tyrants.

* Mary had a teenage pregnancy, which was scandalous in a small town.

* Her fiancé Joseph was ready to separate from his bride except for an angelic visit.

* Family and friends insisted that he was crazy for staying with her.

* A barnyard birth on a cold night was Jesus's welcome.

THE NOT-SO-PERFECT FAMILY WAS THE PERFECT PLACE FOR JESUS TO ARRIVE.

#REDLETTERADVENT

* Herod's jealous decree resulted in a desperate escape to Egypt as refugees.

* A prophecy that this tiny baby's life would end with a violent death for sins he didn't commit.

The not-so-perfect family was the perfect place for Jesus to arrive. That's some good news for all of us.[14]

BUT TAKE HEART!

Jesus handles you with care and brings peace to you in your messiness. Before Jesus died, he wanted to bring peace to his disciples through prayer, advice, warnings, and encouragement. Jesus didn't keep his followers from going through difficulties. The hard times still came. But he assured them they could have peace as they went through the painful times of life.

Yesterday, I introduced John 16:33 to you. Today, let's break down Jesus's words further:

> **"I have told you these things, so that in me you may have peace. In this world you will have trouble. But take heart! I have overcome the world."**

Jesus's peace does not equal ease. He didn't say that once you believe in him, you'll never experience hardship. Not only did Jesus predict hard moments, but he also got down into the mess and lived that hard life right alongside you.

> **"In this world, you will have tribulation."**

Our king wasn't born in a royal court but a rugged cradle. No other religion has a God who humbled himself; who knows what it's like to be abandoned by friends, crushed by injustice, tortured, and killed.

Other religions' teachings deal with the problem of suffering by directly connecting it to how good or bad you are. But not Jesus. He was perfect, and yet he suffered terribly.

Jesus warned that while we would also be in these kinds of complex situations, we would not have to lose peace.

"In me, you may have peace."

It's not the good people who are in and the wrong people who are out. **Everyone who believes is in by the grace of Jesus Christ.** Christmas says that God has walked through the darkness you are in now and worse. So, you can trust him because he gets it and will give you inner peace in an awful situation.

"But take heart!"

Jesus tells us to take heart. Another way of saying this is, "Take courage!" "Be bold!" or "Have good cheer!" Amid your not-so-perfect times, you can have peace because God is not only with us; he truly understands us.

"I have overcome the world."

To understand Christmas is to understand the basic Christian message: Jesus Christ came into this world to save sinners, including you and me. He overcame all the things that created conflict in the world. You can decide to go into some uncomfortable conflict when everyone else gets out of there. You know Jesus has already defeated it.

This Christmas, take heart when sweaters are itchy, dogs poop in the wrong places, and the weather is less than ideal. Be bold when Christmas isn't living up to the expectations you have. Have good cheer, knowing that even if nothing this season is going how you had hoped, you are still at peace with the God of the universe.

Even when you are a less-than-perfect family, you have a more-than-perfect God!

UNBOX YOUR PEACE TODAY.

CHALLENGE DAY 11
PEACE: HANDLE WITH CARE

Many people don't reveal their struggles because they are never asked. Take time today to ask someone how they are doing and listen. Just having someone listen can bring peace to someone in a stressful situation. If you are the one who needs to be handled with care, reach out to someone you trust and share how you are feeling.

DAY 12

PEACE:

DELIVERED

"GLORY TO GOD IN THE HIGHEST, AND ON EARTH PEACE AMONG THOSE WITH WHOM HE IS PLEASED!" (LUKE 2:14, ESV).

BIRTH ANNOUNCEMENTS

Our oldest son, Nathan, was born on October 22nd, 2007. Knowing his due date was around Halloween, Allison bought a tiny hot dog costume with the idea that she would dress our newborn up and announce his arrival to the world, Halloween style. The plan worked! Alongside the adorable picture of our tiny baby boy in a hotdog costume were the words "Happy Halloweenie!" with his name, date of birth, height, and weight.

By the time our second son was born in 2010, social media had taken over that job. The rise of social media has given way to several opportunities for people to celebrate a new birth. There's the pregnancy announcement post, the gender reveal post, and still, of course, the birth announcement!

Jesus's birth announcement wasn't well received. Life may have been entirely different for people in the ancient world, but judgment and criticism haven't changed throughout history. I'm sure Jesus's mother, Mary, felt judged. If she had lived today, Mary's pregnancy post would have caused quite a frenzy on social media.

First, pregnancy outside of marriage would have led to a string of negative comments and discussions. Second, she didn't need to wait for the 20-week ultrasound to throw a gender reveal party. No one would have believed that an angel visited Mary and told her that she would have a baby boy. People would whisper behind her back, "*Who, exactly, does she think she is?*"

Finally, Mary had nothing to do with the birth announcement either. We have a record of the baby announcement in the Bible. Charles Schultz's Linus gave a famous recitation of Jesus's birth in a cartoon that people still watch today in *Charlie Brown's Christmas*.

Here's the Bible reading from Luke. (Good luck not reading it in Linus's voice. It's impossible!)

> "**And in the same country shepherds abided in the field, watching their flock by night. And, lo, the angel of the Lord came upon them, and the glory of the Lord shone round about them: and they were sore afraid. And the angel said unto them, Fear not: for, behold, I bring you good tidings of great joy, which shall be to all people. For unto you is born this day in the city of David a Saviour, which is Christ the Lord. And this shall be a sign unto you; Ye shall find the babe wrapped in swaddling clothes, lying in a manger. And suddenly there was with the angel a multitude of the heavenly host praising God, and saying, Glory to God in the highest, and on earth peace, good will toward men.**" (Luke 2:8-14, KJV)

The craziest part of Jesus's birth announcement was the audience.

UNTO THE SHEPHERDS

If we were in charge of Jesus's birth announcement, it would have said something like,

> **"Today, in Bethlehem, to Joseph and Mary of Nazareth, a son, Jesus Christ, was born."**

Then, it would have listed the height and weight of baby Jesus and included a photo.

But Jesus's announcement was different. It said:

> **"For unto you is born this day in the city of David a Saviour, which is Christ the Lord."**

Did you notice that the announcement did not mention Joseph and Mary? The angels said, "unto you." The "you" were the shepherds. God first announced the arrival of baby Jesus to a group of nobodies in Bethlehem. Those guys were shocked. The famous Christmas hymn *The First Noel* describes those shepherds pretty accurately.

> **The First Noel,**
> **The angel did say,**
> **Was to certain poor shepherds**
> **In fields as they lay.**

These shepherds were poor and worked the graveyard shift. They were out in a field, not safe and warm at home. Martin Luther said the shepherds were "despised by and unknown to the world which sleeps in the night...the poor shepherds go about their work at night. They represent all the lowly who live on earth, often despised and unnoticed but dwell only under the protection of heaven."[15]

Not only were they low on the social ladder, but they were physically filthy. The shepherds were constantly in contact with dirty puddles, strong odors, sheep manure, buzzing insects, and blood from the cuts or scrapes of the animals. Clean is not the word you would pick to describe them.

Because the shepherds were familiar with the Torah, the first five Old Testament books, their being physically dirty would have made them ceremonially unclean. According to the Torah, they had to fulfill the Law perfectly to please God. But their profession of herding would have kept them from being able to perform the ritual cleansing. So, they could not worship God properly in the temple or participate in religious events. Nothing was pleasing about these shepherds!

In light of this, I am sure that these shepherds were shocked when the angels appeared. What did they do to deserve that honor?

A CONFUSING (BUT PEACEFUL) ENDING

Jesus's grand birth announcement ended with the following words:

"GLORY TO GOD IN THE HIGHEST, AND ON EARTH PEACE AMONG THOSE WITH WHOM HE IS PLEASED!" (LUKE 2:14, ESV).

That's a thrilling announcement, but I wonder how the shepherds heard it. As you just read, God cannot accept ceremonially unclean people. So, while I'm sure the shepherds would have loved to have God's peace, they assumed it wasn't for them.

We should also be confused. If peace is only among those with whom God is pleased, how do we know if God is pleased with us today?

Until this baby was born in a manger, there was only one way to please God. That was the perfect and complete fulfillment of God's Law. The shepherds rightfully counted themselves out. Their career kept them from ever being clean. You have to count yourselves out, too. You can't keep God's Law perfectly. And yet, God announced this baby to these unclean, unpleasant people.

That's the announcement of Christmas. **Baby Jesus changed everything for everybody.** At that moment, God ushered in a new era. Jesus came to be the perfect fulfillment of the Law. He lived the life that none of us are capable of living. Reread his words from Day Two, found originally in Matthew 5:17-18.

> **"Do not think that I have come to abolish the Law or the Prophets; I have not come to abolish them but to fulfill them. For truly I tell you, until heaven and earth disappear, not the smallest letter, not the least stroke of a pen, will by any means disappear from the Law until everything is accomplished."**

Jesus fulfilled every demand of God's Law, and then, at the end of his life, he died the death that you and I deserve. Not only this, but he rose from the dead, conquering sin, death, and the devil. His peace finally came.

AVAILABLE PEACE

God's peace is now available for you, and as a result, you have faith.

"AND WITHOUT FAITH IT IS IMPOSSIBLE TO PLEASE GOD BECAUSE ANYONE WHO COMES TO HIM MUST BELIEVE THAT HE EXISTS AND THAT HE REWARDS THOSE WHO EARNESTLY SEEK HIM" (HEBREWS 11:6).

God's pleasure is not just for those who check all the boxes and are perfectly clean. His pleasure is toward those who trust in his Son. Sometimes, it's hard to imagine this, but God's face is beaming, bright, and smiling toward you. Just as he accepted his Son,

Jesus, he accepted you. The true Christmas gift was delivered right in your hands.

More than seven centuries before Jesus entered this world on Christmas morning, the prophet Isaiah reminded us of the result of Jesus's mission.

> "I delight greatly in the LORD, my soul rejoices in my God. For he has clothed me with garments of salvation and arrayed me in a robe of his righteousness" (Isaiah 61:10a).

You are pleasing to God because you now get to wear his robes of righteousness. When God the Father looks at you, He looks at you through the lens of what Jesus has done for you. He sees you in the perfect white robes of righteousness (right relationship with God and others). The birth announcement of Christmas is that anyone who is messy can come to Jesus. **Jesus makes the messy clean.**

UNBOX YOUR PEACE TODAY.

CHALLENGE DAY 12
PEACE: DELIVERED

In Isaiah 59:1-3, the prophet clarifies that we are not at peace with God because of our sins. Yet, the message of Christmas morning from today's devotion is that Jesus came to make the messy clean.

> Surely the arm of the Lord is not too short to save,
>   nor his ear too dull to hear.
> But your iniquities have separated
>   you from your God;
> your sins have hidden his face from you,
>   so that he will not hear.

For your hands are stained with blood,
   your fingers with guilt.
Your lips have spoken falsely,
   and your tongue mutters wicked things.

Spend 5-10 minutes writing down sins that have separated you from God. Do this on a separate piece of paper. After writing down all that sin, make the angel's announcement personal for you today. Fill out the verse below with your name inserted. Then, after reading the announcement with your name out loud, rip up the paper that includes your sin into as many pieces as you can and throw it away.

Unto _____ (insert your name), is born this day in the city of David a Savior, who is Christ the Lord.

OPTIONAL CHALLENGE

Over the next few days, watch *Charlie Brown's Christmas*, a great holiday movie with a beautiful message.

DAY 13

PEACE:

RETURNS

"BLESSED ARE THE PEACEMAKERS, FOR THEY SHALL BE CALLED SONS OF GOD" (MATTHEW 5:9).

FAMILY TREE

I come from a family tree that includes four generations of pastors. People are often surprised to hear that. "Wow! What are the odds of four generations of pastors?" they ask.

But it actually shouldn't be that surprising. I'm not sure about four generations back, but research shows that what your father does for a living dramatically influences what you do.

The *Review of Economic Studies Limited* analyzed data and revealed some interesting findings. A father's job has a huge influence. Take a look at the graph below, compiled from Brown University.[16]

DYNASTIC BIAS ACROSS OCCUPATIONS

Occupation	(1) % with father in same occupation	(2) % of fathers in each occupation	(3) Dynastic bias
Federal public administration	7.29	1.74	4.20
Carpenter	14.39	2.72	5.29
Electrician	10.18	1.07	9.53
Dentist	2.56	0.19	13.31
Plumber	12.50	0.85	14.65
Lawyer	10.16	0.57	17.83
Doctor	13.91	0.59	23.73
Economist	1.54	0.04	37.26
Legislator	3.55	0.01	354.06

This chart shows that having a dad in the field raises your likelihood of choosing that same path. From the nine careers listed above, the minimum is that you are 4.2x more likely to jump into that same career. And, if your dad happens to be a legislator, you are 354x more likely to become one yourself. Whoa!

We see this same pattern in sports with the Griffey family in MLB, the Manning family in the NFL, and the Curry and Barry families in the NBA.

And let's not forget moms! A mother's career also makes a significant impact. A nurse's daughter was 3.75 times more likely to become a nurse than the rest of the population.

So, I am an example of dynastic bias. Having a dad as a pastor gave me a greater chance of being a pastor. It should not be such a big surprise after all. Even if you don't choose a career path similar to those in your family, it's obvious how much your family impacts who you are and what you do.

STANDING IN THE CROSSFIRE

If God is our Heavenly Father, then our likelihood of following in Jesus's footsteps should also be high. In the Sermon on the Mount, Jesus talks about how peacemakers are the sons of God.

"BLESSED ARE THE PEACEMAKERS, FOR THEY SHALL BE CALLED SONS OF GOD" (MATTHEW 5:9).

After God gives us his inner peace, he calls us to then be peacemakers in the world. A peace*keeper* avoids any conflict. A peace*maker* shows up in areas of conflict to create peace.

God did not call you to be a peacekeeper. He called you to be a peacemaker. Do you see the difference? Receiving God's peace means you are the perfect candidate to give away or return God's peace to others.

FOUR KINDS OF PEACEMAKERS

When Jesus stood on the mountain and preached that peacemakers would be called sons of God, he addressed a crowd with different ideas for achieving peace. Why did these people have such different ideas of peace? To explore this, we must look at their history and the ruling powers of the day.

A hundred years before Jesus, the Romans had taken over Jerusalem and Judah. They were brutal and ruled with an iron fist. The Jewish people had many different ideas about peace under the Romans. From the Gospels, we see at least four prominent sects of Jews emerge.

See the chart below for information on these four groups, their activities, and how they thought one could make peace.

Jewish Group	What were they known for?	What were their peace-making methods?
Sadducees	High priests, predominantly wealthy, who didn't believe in the resurrection.	They compromised with Roman officials. They made political deals to keep the peace.
Pharisees	The most featured group in the Gospels. They were rule-following legal experts.	They created peace by making lots of rules. They thought that strict regulations would achieve peace.
Essenes	A group of people who lived away from everyone else.	They believed they could find peace by separating themselves from any conflict.
Zealots	A group of hot-headed fighters who opposed anyone who disagreed with them.	They believed peacemaking would come through fighting. They never met an argument that they didn't try to win.

Jesus loved all these people, but he didn't agree with any of their ideas to make peace.

* Jesus didn't make peace by just compromising and making deals.

* Jesus didn't make peace out of adhering to more rules.

* Jesus didn't make peace by hiding out or avoiding conflict.

* Jesus didn't make peace by picking fights with everyone.

If none of these worked for Jesus, they won't work for us either. So, where do we bring peace?

STANDING IN THE MIDDLE

One ideal place for peacemaking is the church. In most churches, you will find people on either side of most cultural issues. The church is filled with people who can unite through Jesus despite differences. It is easy to see peacemaking happen in church.

Outside of church, peacemaking can happen wherever people interact because no two people are alike. Therefore, it is inevitable that they will sometimes disagree. You may find yourself a peacemaker in your extended family, workplace, or home.

However, if you find yourself isolated most of the time, this may be an opportunity for you to discover ways to interact with others. As soon as you do that, you will see opportunities for peacemaking.

While striving to be a peacemaker is noble, it is essential to remember some things that peacemaking isn't.

1 **Peacemaking doesn't mean you have to agree with everyone.** Peacemaking requires a firm belief in Jesus as your Lord and Savior. You must understand and believe in the Bible's teachings about salvation, forgiveness, and heaven. All those things are tools you need to create peace. Without them, you will only be a people-pleaser. And trust me, you will not get very far. I've tried! Rather than making everyone happy, there were times when I ended up being blamed for everything. Jesus once said,

"DO YOU THINK THAT I CAME TO BRING PEACE ON EARTH? NO, I TELL YOU, BUT DIVISION" (LUKE 12:51).

This is very confusing! Why would Jesus say he comes to bring division? Jesus warns us not to follow the flow and support what anyone says. Having a truth means sometimes you will find conflict with those who disagree. Also, we must remember that while his warning includes division, it doesn't end with division. He went to the cross because his ultimate goal was to make peace, but he knew his sacrifice would temporarily bring division. If Jesus's offering brought temporary division, you better believe our efforts to make peace will do the same.

2 **Peacemaking doesn't mean you will never have resistance.** Almost everyone likes the idea of peace, but not everyone will understand your method of peacemaking. Resistance is not always a sign that you are wrong. It could be a sign you are doing something right. Resistance, and even persecution, can come from those who don't think you are bringing peace correctly.

GOD'S CHILDREN BRING PEACE

Jesus found peace by serving others. He didn't try to make a deal with us, give us more rules to live by, sweep all our sins under the rug, or punish and scream at us to get us to cooperate.

He served us by dying for us. His death and resurrection brought hope to us amid conflict. We could not see a way out of our mess. **The key to giving peace to others is to continue receiving God's peace for yourself.**

Now that you have this peace, you can be a peacemaker by serving the people you encounter. The apostle Paul said it this way,

"IF IT IS POSSIBLE, AS FAR AS IT DEPENDS ON YOU, LIVE AT PEACE WITH EVERYONE" (ROMANS 12:18).

The world needs the peace that only God can bring. As sons and daughters of God, you are called to give this peace away. Looking at what God does, you could say peacemaking is the family business.

UNBOX YOUR PEACE TODAY.

CHALLENGE DAY 13
PEACE: RETURNS

Give the peace of God away today. This week, you spent time unboxing God's peace. Now, how can you return that peace to someone else? If you have an unresolved conflict with someone, initiate a text, phone call, or meeting with this person. If you know someone in a highly stressful situation, do something today to serve this person. If you know someone who has a different worldview than you, offer to listen to their story so that you can better understand their perspective. No matter how you return God's peace to others, know that as you give God's peace away, God's peace is going with you.

DAYS

14-19

OF ADVENT

"I HAVE TOLD YOU THESE THINGS SO
THAT YOU WILL BE FILLED WITH MY
JOY. YES, YOUR JOY WILL OVERFLOW!"

LUKE 15:11, NLT

WEEK OF

DAY 14

JOB:

ADD
TO CART

"ASK AND YOU WILL RECEIVE, AND YOUR JOY WILL BE
COMPLETE" (JOHN 16:24B).

GRATEFUL THURSDAY,
GREEDY FRIDAY

What do you want for Christmas this year? I remember my parents repeatedly asking me that every year as a kid. As a society, we can base the success of Christmas on the gifts a person may or may not receive, especially with kids.

I find it sad and ironic that right after our nation celebrates a holiday called Thanksgiving, we follow it up with Black Friday. Thanksgiving Thursday is the day Americans practice more gratitude than any other day. Then, the next day, they practice more greed than any other day of the year. It's typical, then, that this consumeristic, greedy mindset we practice on the day after Thanksgiving carries itself through the Advent season.

French sociologist Jean Baudrillard pointed out that materialism has become the dominant system of meaning in the Western world. He has argued that shopping is a bigger problem than atheism when it comes to cultural Christianity. But is any of it making us any more joyful? The answer is no.

Collectively, Americans have more stuff than ever. An industry that barely existed just over three decades ago, the self-storage industry, is now valued at $58 billion globally, with our nation alone accounting for $44 billion.[17] Even though we buy more stuff, research shows we are collectively becoming less joyful and optimistic.

Thomas Aquinas was an Italian theologian who lived in the 13th century. He was asked what would satisfy our desire to be happy. In other words, what would it take for a human to feel satisfied? Here is the answer he came up with,

> **"Everything. We would have to experience everything and everybody and be experienced by everything and everybody to feel satisfied. Eat at every restaurant; travel to every country, every city, every exotic locale, experience every natural wonder; make love to every partner we could possibly desire; win every award, climb to the top of every field; own every item in the world; etc. We would have to experience it all to ever feel satisfied."[18]**

That seems exhausting, impossible, and undesirable. Surely, there must be some other way to be truly satisfied.

DISORDERED LOVES?

It's okay to buy, receive, or even want gifts. I experience great joy in the giving and receiving of gifts. But any time you place your ultimate joy in created things and not the Creator of those things, you are living with what St. Augustine (another old theologian who lived and wrote just a couple hundred years after Jesus died) calls disordered love. Any time your love of things surpasses your love of God, you'll never be content with what you have. You will never have enough.

If we ought to find our ultimate happiness in God and not material things, why did God make all this tempting stuff? Some people may think it's wise to get rid of our stuff and that we should run away and live in simplicity. But that isn't a call for everyone. Or a person should get rid of all of their junk. Perhaps you should do a good spring (or Advent) cleaning and donate some extra stuff.

Ultimately, God made your stuff to be gifts. He placed them in your world for your enjoyment. They have a purpose. God loves to give you good gifts and encourages you to ask him for good gifts. Hear his words from the Sermon on the Mount.

> **Ask and it will be given to you; seek and you will find; knock and the door will be opened to you. For everyone who asks receives; the one who seeks finds; and to the one who knocks, the door will be opened. Which of you, if your son asks for bread, will give him a stone? Or if he asks for a fish, will give him a snake? If you, then, though you are evil, know how to give good gifts to your children, how much more will your Father in heaven give good gifts to those who ask him! (Matthew 7:7-11)**

While nothing else should ever take the place of God in our lives, it's okay to use the things in this world for our pleasure.

Some might say, "Well, shouldn't I seek the giver of the gifts and not the gifts?"

There's truth behind it, but it's also misleading. For instance, if I said to Allison, "I love you. Therefore, I will not love the meals, the presents, or the time you give me," would that make any sense? No! If I loved the gifts or time more than her, then my love had gotten out of line. But by loving the things she gives or does for me, I am honoring her.

Conversely, John Calvin (a French theologian during the Protestant Reformation) said, "In despising the gifts, we insult the Giver."

The joy is found in the giver of the ultimate gift.

While it's not wrong to experience joy in the gifts of this world, none of them bring lasting and permanent joy. As great as your Christmas gifts might be this year, the odds are that you won't even remember them in years to come.

THE GIMMIE GLEAM

Gifts of this world may fill you with a temporary pleasure, but that pleasure will soon fade. Even if you fully agree with the devotion today, the world still has a strong pull. Advertisers and marketers are good at what they do. Artificial intelligence and algorithms are getting better and better at predicting what you are interested in. You soon begin to get that "gimmie gleam" in your eyes. We all get sucked into the lie that a particular product, vacation, type of food, or experience will change our lives.

C.S. Lewis was a famous writer who wrote about our desires in his book *The Weight of Glory*. In it, he was making the case that we settle too much for created things over the Creator. Here are his words:

> **"We are half-hearted creatures fooling around with drink and sex and ambition when infinite joy is offered us. Like an ignorant child who wants to go on making mud pies in the slum because he cannot imagine what is meant by an offer of a holiday at the sea. We are far too easily pleased."[19]**

The ultimate question is, where do you look for ultimate joy?

MOST SATISFIED

Will you settle for less than what God wants to give you? Not only did Jesus encourage us to ask for good gifts in the Sermon on the Mount, but later, his words spoken to his disciples remind us that the ultimate joy is in him. John 16:24b says, **"Ask and you will receive, and your joy will be complete."** Our joy is completed in Jesus.

Pastor John Piper once said something I've remembered for the last 20 years. He said, "God is most glorified when I am most satisfied in him." Are you most satisfied with Jesus?

I hope you experience great temporary joy in giving and receiving gifts of all kinds this Christmas season. But remember that the greatest gift, the only one that can fill you with everlasting joy, is Jesus.

UNBOX YOUR JOY TODAY.

CHALLENGE DAY 14

JOY: ADD TO CART

Write down the top five things that bring you joy.

1. Church events
2. Friends & family
3.
4.
5.

While there are many ways that God gives joy to you, it's important to remember that all joy ultimately comes from God. He should always be at the top of the list. Go to **www.redletterchallenge.com/adventverses** and read the ten Bible verses on joy. Write down and memorize one of the Bible verses as you unbox joy.

DAY 15

JOY:

CHECKOUT

> BUT THE ANGEL SAID TO THEM, "DO NOT BE AFRAID. I BRING YOU GOOD NEWS THAT WILL CAUSE GREAT JOY FOR ALL THE PEOPLE" (LUKE 2:10).

GETTING THE GIGGLES

When I describe great joy to you, what comes to mind? For me, nothing displays great joy like laughter. *Psychology Today* informs us that four-year-old's laugh three hundred times a day, whereas the average forty-year-old only laughs four times a day.[20] Life inevitably becomes more serious as you age, but I don't think more decades of life should make us laugh seventy-five times less.

Today, I'll share why laughter is important and how those who unbox Jesus Christ and his gifts, no matter what age you might be, can lead the way with the joy of laughter.

LAUGHTER IS THE BEST MEDICINE

There are many places where modern-day science is catching up to what the Bible has taught. Proverbs 17:22 says,

"A cheerful heart is good medicine." As the saying goes, "Laughter is the best medicine."

The first reason we laugh is because it's good for us.

Several studies on laughter show the benefits of what laughter can do for you. Read some of them below.[21]

* Laughter increases the longevity of your life.

* Laughter relieves pain and stress.

* Laughter makes you 40% less likely to have a heart attack.

* Laughter stimulates your immune system to help fight off diseases.

* Laughter triggers the right side of the brain, which releases creativity and helps you make better decisions.

This gift of laughter has far more physical, emotional, mental, and relational benefits. Reason number one is enough to make sure we keep laughing in this world! Not only is laughing good for you, but it can also help others.

CHANGING THE NARRATIVE

Christians are not always known for their positive words. According to the book *UnChristian* by authors David Kinnamon and Gabe Lyons, some of the top words that describe Christians today are old-fashioned, boring, and out of touch with reality.[22]

It's time we change that narrative. What if laughter is the answer?

When the Israelites from the Old Testament were released from 70 years of captivity in Babylon, they were filled with laughter and sang for joy. In response to seeing their outer joy, *"The other nations said, 'What amazing things the Lord has done for them'"* (Psalm 126:3, NLT).

The second reason we laugh is because laughing is a good witness to others.

When we carry the joy of the Lord with us, especially through our laughter, we become an incredible witness that others notice and are intrigued by.

Like the Israelites, Jesus invited us into this reality in his words in the Sermon on the Mount. Jesus said,

> **"In the same way, let your light shine before others, that they may see your good deeds and glorify your Father in heaven" (Matthew 5:16).**

If we are serious about our witness to others, especially during Advent, our actions must match our beliefs. **The birth of Jesus brings great joy to the world.**

D. L. Moody said, "If Christians are gloomy and cast down, and not full of praise, the world will reject their Gospel. It is not good news if it does not produce praise in those who have it. Praise, joy, and laughter are a big part of our witness to the world."[23]

No matter what you may have been taught or how you were raised, it's okay for Christians to have a good time in this world. His enemies criticized Jesus for partying with sinners. He believed it was good to celebrate at weddings and enjoy the hospitality of his friends.

People could criticize you for enjoying your life as a follower of Christ, but I believe far more will find your joy contagious. One pastor said, "A Lord who never gives laughter to his people is not appealing, but is appalling."[24] In Advent, God has allowed you to laugh no matter what this world brings.

GETTING THE LAST LAUGH

Reread the angel's proclamation.

> **"But the angel said to them, 'Do not be afraid. I bring you good news that will cause great joy for all the people'"** (Luke 2:10).

The news the angel was about to share is the cause of great joy.

> **"The Savior—yes, the Messiah, the Lord—has been born today in Bethlehem, the city of David!"** (Luke 2:11, NLT).

You can laugh because Jesus delivered on every promise he's ever made. You can fully trust that all of God's promises are coming true.

The third reason we laugh is because Jesus is good news.

We who once were dead, according to our sins, are now alive again through Jesus. The Protestant Reformer Martin Luther once said, **"The Gospel is nothing less than laughter and joy."**

Did you know there is an old Greek Orthodox tradition that the church gathers to tell jokes and laugh on the Sunday following Easter? Laughter was their way of celebrating the big joke God played on Satan. Satan thought the cross was his victory, but it spelled his doom instead. It was the most serious business of all history, and yet it was the basis for laughter because God used Satan's greatest evil to accomplish his own greatest good. This is why you can laugh!

I know that not everything in this world is as it ought to be. You'll spend more time reading about this as you continue to unbox joy in future days. You can trust, however, that no matter what comes at you, God will use it for his good and always get the last laugh!

Amid a psalm about nations conspiring against God, there is this beautiful gem of a verse in Psalm 2:4a: **"The One enthroned in heaven laughs."**

Right now, God is seated on his throne and laughing. Jesus has already completed the rescue mission. He laughs because he can see the whole picture, which ends well. No matter how much sorrow this fallen world brings to you personally, there will be eternal rejoicing and laughter. God's people will have the last laugh, which will never end!

UNBOX YOUR JOY TODAY.

CHALLENGE DAY 15
JOY: CHECKOUT

Have a chuckle today. Say Jesus's words five times to yourself:

> **"I have told you these things so that you will be filled with my joy. Yes, your joy will overflow!" (Luke 15:11, NLT).**

In light of the overflowing joy that Jesus has already given us, do something today that will bring joy and laughter to your life. Laugh, knowing that the victory has already been won!

OPTIONAL CHALLENGE

Nearly everyone has a list of favorite Christmas movies, many of which might bring great laughter. Gather the family, pop some popcorn, and enjoy your favorite Christmas movie.

DAY 16

JOY:

IN TRANSIT

"AS SOON AS THE SOUND OF YOUR GREETING REACHED MY EARS, THE BABY IN MY WOMB LEAPED FOR JOY" (LUKE 1:44).

JOYFULLY WAITING

For some, the thing they most fondly remember about a vacation, a party, or receiving a gift is not the event itself but the anticipation of it. The anticipation can be the best part if you have something incredible waiting for you.

If you believe that Jesus not only died on the cross but will be returning, you have a lot to look forward to. But I've also found that waiting for something great is hard. You are in the middle. Things will eventually improve, but you don't always see it in the present tense. So, when it comes to joy, you are joyful because of what Jesus has done, and you are joyful that he is returning to make things right.

But how do you have joy right now in the middle? If there's anyone who knows what it's like to be in the middle, it's John the Baptist.

THE SAINT OF JOY

The Old Testament is the story of history, beginning with creation and humankind's fall. Alongside the fall, there was also a promise that one would come to rescue and bring all of humanity back into a right relationship with God. The New Testament is the story of Jesus accomplishing this task through his miraculous birth, life, ministry, death, resurrection, and ascension.

John prepared the way for Jesus. He's the bridge (the middle) between the Old and New Testaments. His job was to announce that the middle was over—Jesus had finally come. In the Catholic tradition, John the Baptist is the patron saint of spiritual joy. This surprised me because my mind doesn't necessarily jump to John when I think of joy.

Zechariah and Elizabeth had been waiting decades to conceive and have a child. Despite their efforts, it just wasn't happening. Then, in their old age, an angel brings joy-filled news to this couple, telling them they will give birth to someone who will play an integral role in announcing the world's Savior.

"HE WILL BE A JOY AND DELIGHT TO YOU, AND MANY WILL REJOICE BECAUSE OF HIS BIRTH, FOR HE WILL BE GREAT IN THE SIGHT OF THE LORD" (LUKE 1:14-15A).

They had waited so long, and the reality of what they would experience was even more significant than they could have imagined. Not only would Mary give birth to a son, but this son had a great anointing from the very beginning. Here is the message that they received about John.

> "He will be filled with the Holy Spirit even before he is born. He will bring back many of the people of Israel to the Lord their God. And he will go on before the Lord, in the spirit and power of Elijah, to turn the hearts

and parents to their children and the disobedient to the wisdom of the righteous—to make ready a people prepared for the Lord" (Luke 1:15b-1:17).

According to the verses above, the Holy Spirit was already alive and active in John before he was born! As further evidence, this same Spirit was about to stir John to do something astoundingly joyful while he was still in the womb.

JOY JUMPS

While they were both pregnant, Elizabeth visited Mary. Read about how this visit started below.

> At that time Mary got ready and hurried to a town in the hill country of Judea, where she entered Zechariah's home and greeted Elizabeth. When Elizabeth heard Mary's greeting, the baby leaped in her womb, and Elizabeth was filled with the Holy Spirit. In a loud voice she exclaimed: "Blessed are you among women, and blessed is the child you will bear! But why am I so favored, that the mother of my Lord should come to me? As soon as the sound of your greeting reached my ears, the baby in my womb leaped for joy. Blessed is she who has believed that the Lord would fulfill his promises to her!" (Luke 1:39-45)

From the first moment John the Baptist was in Jesus's presence, he was leaping for joy! It must have been this joy-filled jump in the womb that cemented John as the patron saint of joy. This passage reveals that the Holy Spirit is undoubtedly a gift given by God. This gift comes to you without any earning or deserving of your own. You can rejoice knowing this gift is inside any and all who say and believe, "Jesus is Lord."

When I read about the life John would continue to live, it's tempting to think, "Well, if I knew God's purpose for my life as clearly as John, then I could live up to it as well. I don't always know what to do." You may be like me and not always feel your purpose is clear. It's hard to feel joyful when confused about what you are ultimately here for.

But let me tell you this: your purpose in this world is the same as John's. **You are here to point people to Jesus.** Just as the Holy Spirit filled John with purpose, he does the same for you today.

SUPPORTING STARS

As John lived out his calling, he experienced great success. He didn't find people; they went to him in the wilderness. He gathered a large following, and many even claimed he was the long-awaited one. It's crazy that as he was trying to point people to Jesus, people confused him to be Jesus instead. This response could have gone to his head. It may have led to accolades, worldly influence, and wealth. But John never let it get to his head.

When people came ready to honor John as the Messiah, he set them straight. He refused to be the show's star and instead joyfully fulfilled his role as a supporting actor. After all, Jesus was the one to watch. John may have had center stage for a while but he never wanted to be the star. Along this line of thinking, John's most famous words are from John 3:30. He said, **"I must decrease, he must increase."**

So, whenever Jesus came, John knew it was time to slip off the stage quietly. Jesus would grow up and claim that no one was greater born of woman than John. Eventually, John was martyred for his faith. The world would say that is a sad ending, but John and all those killed for their faith in Jesus know that whatever suffering they experience will one day be glorified in eternity.

Unlike John, many people today are more concerned about their following than following Christ. There is nothing wrong with your success. You or a family member may have had a center-stage presence at some point, but remember, you are not the star. Jesus is. The most significant test of your character is not always a struggle but what happens and who you become when life brings success. You can find joy in being the supporting actor for what Christ is doing.

The apostle Paul speaks about this truth. **"I consider that our present sufferings are not worth comparing with the glory that will be revealed in us"** (Romans 8:17).

No matter what the world brings, we can have joy. Because of Jesus, even the worst of what the world can offer to us, death itself, will not have the final say. John teaches us that we can have joy as we play a supporting role to the one who is the bright, shining star.

UNBOX YOUR JOY TODAY.

CHALLENGE DAY 16
JOY: IN TRANSIT

Have a Simple Joys Day! John was imprisoned for his faith in Jesus, but that didn't stop him from being the patron saint of joy. You can experience joy no matter what your worldly experiences are.

List out ten simple, little things that make you smile. Some of mine are eating Asian food with Nathan, shooting hoops with Brady, working out with Allison, watching football with my extended family, and relaxing in my leather recliner. After you write out your ten, try to experience as many of them as possible today.

1 _____   **6** _____

2 _____   **7** _____

3 _____   **8** _____

4 _____   **9** _____

5 _____   **10** _____

DAY 17

JOY:

HANDLE
WITH CARE

"BLESSED ARE THOSE WHO MOURN, FOR THEY WILL BE
COMFORTED" (MATTHEW 5:4).

HARD QUESTIONS

I know everything in your life isn't perfect and filled with laughter all the time. As we've already stated, sometimes the season we are in amplifies not just the good times, but the heartbreaks. We all have times when we need to be handled with care.

Many Christians wrongly believe that if they suffer, then perhaps they are either doing something wrong or even that God may be punishing them. The truth is that a life spent in pursuit of Jesus comes with promises that you will experience suffering, trouble, and hardship in this world. Though filled with hope, peace, joy, and love from Jesus, the world we live in right now is still filled with sorrow and grief. Sin is still prevalent in the world we live in.

Anytime sin is around; hard questions will be right around the corner. How can you have joy despite all of life's difficulties? Is it even possible?

UNCOMFORTABLE COMFORT

I have a weird relationship with the word "comfort." Biblically, God promises comfort to those in a relationship with him, but I misappropriate it more than any other word.

If you ask me about my ideal future self, where my family would be ten to twenty years from now, I am far more comfortable in every future vision I give you. I am more prosperous, have more time to enjoy my hobbies, and continue to celebrate my marriage and the success of my kids (and hopefully their marriages with their kids at that point!) In none of my ideal visions, am I fighting or contending for my faith, suffering for the Gospel, or dependent on daily provision from God. In other words, I long for a life of comfort.

As lovely as it seems, as a follower of Jesus, something about that longing feels off. If you were to boil it down, it's fair to say that the idol of comfort could be the strongest pull I will fight. And I don't think I'm alone.

When pursuing the comfort that this world can bring becomes your primary pursuit, you will tend to do anything and everything possible to avoid discomfort, especially suffering.

So, what do we make of the comfort Jesus promises for those who are mourning?

PARAKALEO

Jesus's words leave us with some clear clues.

"BLESSED ARE THOSE WHO MOURN, FOR THEY WILL BE COMFORTED" (MATTHEW 5:4).

The original Greek language uses the root word *parakaleo*, which we translate as "comforted." The prefix *para* typically means alongside, and the verb *kaleo* means "to be called up or summoned." This word means that when you are mourning, you will have someone to be called up alongside you.

In those days, the noun *parakleton* had a legal connotation, meaning "a helper in court." It has been synonymous throughout history with "advocate," "helper," and "counselor." Jesus even used this word four times in his prayer in John 14-16 to describe the Holy Spirit. Once, in 1 John 2:1, it was used to describe Jesus himself.

Jesus proclaimed that while he would soon ascend to be our "paraclete" in heaven, he would call up the Holy Spirit to bring us help, comfort, and aid right here and now. So, his presence is always close to us.

Christmas is when Jesus was called to be our paraclete. That is the message of the Advent season.

When you mourn, you have Jesus, who has been called up alongside you to help.

Jesus has done his job through birth, ministry, death, resurrection, and ascension. Not only this, but you also have the Holy Spirit inside of you. So, when you mourn, you do not need to chase anything far away or struggle with where to find Jesus. He's right here, not only by our side, as our friend, but inside of us through the Holy Spirit.

Jesus's message is that in the middle of suffering, you can look to him, experience the comfort of the Holy Spirit, and receive empathy from him, who withstood the ultimate suffering on your behalf. In the middle of suffering, Jesus enters as our paraclete.

Jesus is unafraid to enter into the worst parts of your life. The invitation this Advent season is to invite Jesus into even the worst parts of your story. The parts that you don't want anyone to enter. So, whether it's the broken promise, the eating disorder, the affair, the overdose, the divorce, the abuse you experienced as a child, the rape, the abortion, whatever it may be, there is NOTHING too dark for Jesus. He is calling you into that darkness to get you through that darkness. You can bring your worst to Jesus because Jesus has already brought his best to you.[25]

When something goes awry in this world, the great news of the Christmas season is that you don't have to look far. You have a paraclete in Jesus that you can look to and turn your eyes to at any time.

If anyone knows this truth, it's Helen Lemmel.

TURN YOUR EYES

Helen Lemmel was a hymn writer. One of her most well-known hymns is *Turn Your Eyes Upon Jesus*. The song was written and published in the United Kingdom in 1918. This was a challenging year for both the world and for Helen.

In 1918, two significant disruptions occurred worldwide. First, World War I was still underway. Second, a major global pandemic, the Spanish Flu, struck the world. Between 50 and 100 million people died, and the United Kingdom was one of the worst-hit places.

While the world had its issues, Helen also suffered profound personal loss. Her husband divorced her, citing that his main reason for doing so was because she was losing her sight and going blind. So, during worldwide disruption and loss, and in the middle of feeling the weight of being alone and not physically being able to see anything, she writes these words:

> **And turn your eyes upon Jesus**
> **Look full in His wonderful face**
> **And the things of earth will grow strangely dim**
> **In the light of His glory and grace[26]**

This woman is an incredible example of faith. She shows us that the worst of this world can come after us, and yet, as we keep our eyes fixed on Jesus, all of the worst grows strangely dim. No matter what comes your way, even when you can't see, you can still keep your eyes fixed on Jesus and find joy.

UNBOX YOUR JOY TODAY.

CHALLENGE DAY 17
JOY: HANDLE WITH CARE

Read the following verses that describe our paraclete, the One who has been called alongside you. After reading these verses, go alongside someone who needs a friend this season. If that person is you, contact someone you know and ask for help.

- ✳ John 14:16

- ✳ John 14:26

- ✳ John 15:26

- ✳ John 16:7

- ✳ 1 John 2:1

DAY 18

JOY:

DELIVERED

"WHEN THEY SAW THE STAR, THEY WERE OVERJOYED"
(MATTHEW 2:10).

CANADIAN PANDA SOCKS

What's the weirdest gift you've ever received? There's a popular expression used this time of year when opening gifts. You've all heard it before.

"It's the thought that counts."

But I don't think that's true. One year, I received a pair of socks. There's nothing wrong with a pair of socks. They were dress socks. Cool, I can go with that. Printed on the socks were pandas. Not only did the socks feature pandas, but on the top, the socks had the word Canada written on top.

Let me go on record to say that I have nothing against either the panda or the nation of Canada. Pandas are cool. And I know a couple of people from Canada who are fantastic. I just never expected to get a pair of socks with Canadian pandas. Is that even a thing? Let me just say that Canadian panda socks weren't on my gift request list for that year. So, when I opened the gift, I probably looked a little off-kilter and may have said, "Huh." Finally, someone in the room said, "Well, it's the thought that counts, right?"

Today, I want to unpack some of the gifts Jesus received. I want you to ponder what thoughts went behind the three famous gifts delivered to Jesus by the Magi. What caused them to pick those specific gifts? It is one thing to travel a long distance, but it's another to travel a long distance to deliver particular gifts. What were they all about?

Matthew only gives us a little detail about the offering of these gifts. Read his account below.

> **"On coming to the house, they saw the child with his mother, Mary, and they bowed down and worshiped him. Then they opened their treasures and presented him with gifts of gold, frankincense, and myrrh"** (Matthew 2:11).

These seem like bizarre gifts to give anyone, especially a newborn or toddler. Do these gifts fall into weird categories like Canadian panda socks? Or is there some thought behind each of these gifts that can help us gain greater understanding of who Jesus is?

UNBOXING GOLD, FRANKINCENSE, AND MYRRH

FRANKINCENSE

According to essential oil experts, frankincense is the Swiss Army Knife of oils.[27] It has lots of purposes. According to the *International Journal of Nutrition, Pharmacology, and Neurological Diseases*, frankincense oil possesses antiseptic, astringent, carminative, diarrhetic, digestive, sedative, uterine, and vulnerary therapeutic properties.[28]

That sounds impressive! While I don't know what half of it means, frankincense is a costly and practical gift that helps heal sicknesses and treat wounds. Its primary purpose is medicinal today, but it also had a spiritual purpose in biblical times.

In the Old Testament, frankincense was the oil the priests used during their sacrifices. There were many specific, rigorous details of what a high priest had to do during the sacrifice to help all the people become ceremonially clean from the sins they had collectively committed. We are not discussing cleanliness like a bath with soap but a spiritual cleansing. Frankincense was the critical ingredient in all those sacrifices and would always fill the air during those ceremonies. Therefore, scholars all agree that frankincense represents Jesus as our High Priest.[29]

When the Magi delivered frankincense, it was for more than just to heal his eventual aches and pains. **Frankincense was delivered to Jesus to acknowledge that he is our High Priest.**

MYRRH

This is the gift that is least commonly known in our world today. It seems like a strange gift. So, what is myrrh? Myrrh is a valuable gum-like substance used seventeen times in the Bible.[30] You can buy frankincense for around $100 for just 15mL, but myrrh has five times the value of frankincense.[31]

Myrrh had many purposes. Along with frankincense, myrrh was used as an ingredient in anointing oil. In the sacrificial system, not only did the high priest need anointing oil, but they would need an innocent animal as well. When the high priest combined the oil (mixed with frankincense and myrrh) with the innocent animal and went through the sacrificial rite, it paid for the sins of the Israelite people.

However, the most common use of myrrh was to embalm the dead. So, myrrh would have been used on Jesus to prepare his body for burial.

Unlike temporary sacrifices made by the high priests, the gift of myrrh declared Jesus to be the eternal sacrifice to pay for the sins of the entire world! Scholars agree that this gift represents Jesus as the Lamb of God, who takes away the sin of the world

When the Magi delivered myrrh, it was for more than a temporary sacrifice. **Myrrh was delivered to Jesus to acknowledge that he is the Lamb of God.**

GOLD

Because of its scarcity and value, gold has been a fitting gift for a king—not just any king, but the greatest King of Kings.

Jesus is a king unlike any other. He came in a very unusual way. People were expecting a king, but not a king like Jesus. In our day, he would have been born in a palace and placed in a crib with purple and gold lining. He'd grow up wearing Gucci onesies and Nike SB Dunk Low Travis Scott shoes. No one expected King Jesus to be born in a cave beside farm animals.

And no one could have ever imagined an innocent king eventually beaten, whipped, and stripped naked to die on a cross. A great king would not have died a shameful criminal's death. Then, after being embalmed with myrrh and buried in a tomb, he rose three days later to rise triumphantly from the grave.

Least of all, no one could have imagined that this king would not only have defeated death, the devil, and sin but would now sit at the right hand of God the Father Almighty with a promise to return.

When the Magi delivered gold, it was more than a costly gift. **Gold was delivered to Jesus to acknowledge his power as the King of Kings.**

It is not the thought that counts. It's the gift that counts.

THE GIFT THAT COUNTS

I'm sure that Mary and Joseph did not have these three gifts on their registry! These gifts are more than just lovely presents to bless a young family. As we have just read, they announced three things about Jesus and his role:

1 Jesus is our High Priest who goes before God the Father to advocate for us.

2 Jesus is our Lamb of God who takes away the world's sins.

3 Jesus is our King of Kings who defeated the worst enemy and promised to return for all those who believe in him.

The Magi were overjoyed to give Jesus their gifts. As you look at the gifts of the Magi, are you compelled to lay a gift at Jesus's manger this Christmas? What's a gift fit for a king, a high priest, and the lamb of God?

Truthfully, there is nothing you have that God wants or needs. The very Gospel is that you are not asked to bring your gift to Jesus but to receive instead the gifts he has for you. You will experience the greatest joy when you receive Jesus as the only gift you need. **Jesus is the gift that counts!**

UNBOX YOUR JOY TODAY.

CHALLENGE DAY 18
JOY: DELIVERED

Unbox these three gifts personally today. Thank God as you go through each gift with prayer.

FRANKINCENSE:

Read Hebrews 4:14-16. Give thanks to Jesus for being your high priest so you can confidently approach God.

MYRRH:

Read 1 Peter 1:17-21. Give thanks to Jesus for being the sacrificial lamb of God that has taken away your sin.

GOLD:

Read 1 Timothy 6:11-16. Give thanks to Jesus for being your King of Kings that will forever reign with you.

DAY 19

JOY:

RETURNS

> "I HAVE TOLD YOU THIS SO THAT MY JOY MAY BE IN YOU AND THAT YOUR JOY MAY BE COMPLETE" (JOHN 15:11)

NOT-SO-MERRY COFFEE

Do you ever use the word "merry" outside of Christmas? I don't think about this word except in this season. Ironically, for as little as we use this word, a large segment of those who believe in Jesus come out of the woodwork to ensure we keep using this word attached to Jesus's birthday.

The word merry is a synonym for joy, so exploring the phrase "Merry Christmas" fits very well to end our unboxing of joy.

Over the past decade, businesses, stores, and individuals have switched from saying "Merry Christmas" to "Happy Holidays" to be more inclusive of all people and religions. This change has created quite a stir! Starbucks officially joined this camp in 2015. Before that, Starbucks unveiled new Christmas-designed cups every year. However, in 2015, Starbucks went with a more minimal design and released a plain red cup with its green and white logo.

Not only did the cups remove any Christmas-related language or artwork, but the rumor was that baristas could no longer wish their customers a Merry Christmas. As a result, a segment of Christians were in an uproar. Some people went so far as to boycott the establishment. One Christian pranked the barista by typing her name as "Mary Christmas" so that the worker would have to say "Merry Christmas" out loud when her cup was ready.

This Starbucks controversy is almost ten years old, but the battle to keep Christ in Christmas rages on. As I reflected on the collective response to this plain red cup and the Church's fight for Christmas, I was secretly embarrassed at how Christians reacted to such scenarios. Why is our first response to asking, "What's wrong with them?" rather than beginning conversations with "How can I listen?" or "How can I help?" On top of all that, a lot of the people we get angry with aren't even Christ followers in the first place!

JOY IS YOUR JOB

It's not Starbucks' job to tell people "Merry Christmas." God didn't ask Starbucks to be this world's light or the earth's salt. It's their job to serve quality coffee. And while some would disagree on their quality, their numbers and revenues prove they are doing just that.

Starbucks never signed up to follow Jesus or to live by his rules, so we can't hold them accountable for something they never signed up for in the first place. Ultimately, we have a God whose first reaction to those outside our fold is not to condemn them but to give grace.

"FOR GOD DID NOT SEND HIS SON INTO THE WORLD TO CONDEMN THE WORLD, BUT TO SAVE THE WORLD THROUGH HIM" (JOHN 3:17).

It's getting more complicated in our country in how to stand firm with our Christian morals and beliefs. Rather than jumping on the negative train and blaming everyone else for what is wrong, I embrace the time and place in which I live. Christians in this country have never been as valuable as we are right now because, in the midst of all of the chaos and confusion, we are left with the only answer that matters! His name is Jesus!

Don't get bothered when other people, businesses, or organizations don't say "Merry Christmas," especially if they don't believe in Christ. There are more significant issues at stake. As for you, go ahead and wish everyone you meet a "Merry Christmas!" But here's my plea: don't just say "Merry Christmas," live it out.

Far more important than saying a phrase, we can return the joy of Jesus in a season and every day of our lives! Too many Christians aren't known as joyful but grumpy. Pastor Billy Graham said that a grumpy Christian is a contradiction in terms. Pope Francis agreed with this sentiment: "A Christian without joy is either not a Christian or he is sick." **A healthy Christian is a joyful Christian.**

 Look at many of the Christmas songs you sing, and you'll find them filled with joy. In the verses of *O Come, All Ye Faithful*, you sing words like "joyful and triumphant," "sing in exultation," and "born this happy morning." You will rock out to the hymn *Joy to the World*. Look into the words of these songs. They tell the story of a God that loves you so much. You were created by God, loved by him, redeemed through his sacrifice, empowered by his Holy Spirit, and assured of heaven with eternal life in his presence.

The world may be filled with difficulty right now, but in Jesus, you have so much to be joyful about. The world needs your voice more than ever. It is time for those who have unboxed Jesus to stop assuming it's someone else's job and take it up ourselves.

JESUS IS JOY!

The Bible is full of happy people.

* The wise men were overwhelmed with joy.

* John the Baptist leaped for joy in the womb in the presence of Jesus.

* The shepherds heard the news, which brought great joy to all the people.

But people forget that Jesus is the happiest of all. Randy Alcorn pointed out, "Ask a random group of believers, 'Who is the happiest human being who ever lived?' and very few, if any, would give the correct answer: Jesus."[32]

Jesus experienced God's Kingdom here on Earth. He healed the sick and the lepers and befriended the outcasts. Jesus welcomed people who never had a chance in this world to the most thrilling ride, to follow after him. He fed the hungry, clothed the naked, and controlled creation. What about any of that isn't joyful? People spread rumors about Jesus being a drunkard and a glutton. How did he get that reputation? By going to parties and festivals. Jesus loves to party! His first miracle was turning water into wine. He used irony and wit in his teachings. And he loved to be around and near the joy of children.

Not only did Jesus experience all of this happiness himself, but he wants to share it with others. You experience an inner joy that many in this world are longing for. That's why Jesus once said to his disciples, **"My food is to do the will of him who sent me and to finish his work"** (John 4:34).

When others think they'll experience joy and fulfillment from the things of this world, Jesus argues that what fills him up most is just doing his job, even when it's brutally hard.

In the Garden of Gethsemane, Jesus knew that a brutal death by crucifixion was awaiting him. In the pain and agony of the moment, Jesus cried out, **"Father, if you are willing, take this cup from me; yet not my will, but yours be done"** (Luke 22:42).

Although this doesn't look like a joyful moment on the outside, the result of that suffering, death followed by resurrection, was pure joy. Joy isn't always easy, but it is possible, no matter what.

Jesus gives you this joy. He said, **"I have told you this so that my joy may be in you and that your joy may be complete"** (John 15:11).

When his joy is inside of us, then we are the most joyful people we can be! Don't just have a "Merry Christmas," be merry every day of your life.

UNBOX YOUR JOY TODAY.

CHALLENGE DAY 19
JOY: RETURNS

Give a joy-filled gift away. God has given you gifts that bring you great joy. Share the joy of Jesus with the world. Giving gifts brings joy not only to the receiver but also to the giver. It could be as simple as buying a coffee for the next person in line or blessing someone in need with a financial gift.

OPTIONAL CHALLENGE

Be overwhelmingly generous to one person. I am borrowing this idea from a friend of mine. Several days before Christmas, he invites many friends for breakfast. He instructs each of them to bring a $100 bill. At the end of the meal, they all give the server $100 as a tip. Every year, the server is overwhelmed with joy.

DAYS
20-25
✦
OF ADVENT

"AS I HAVE LOVED YOU, SO YOU MUST LOVE ONE ANOTHER. BY THIS EVERYONE WILL KNOW THAT YOU ARE MY DISCIPLES, IF YOU LOVE ONE ANOTHER."

JOHN 13:34B-35

WEEK OF

LOVE

DAY 20 ♡

LOVE:

ADD
TO CART

"LOVE IS PATIENT, LOVE IS KIND. IT DOES NOT ENVY, IT DOES
NOT BOAST, IT IS NOT PROUD" (1 CORINTHIANS 13:4).

FORGOTTEN LOVE

In our enthusiasm and eagerness to find love, adding the wrong things to our cart is
easy. Through the gifts of hope, peace, and joy, you have learned that while there are
many good options, Jesus is always the best. It's the same with love. Today, you will
compare an engaged couple to an eager young church. Both were adding good things
to their carts but forgetting Jesus's love.

In 2007, the year Zach and I got married, Zach's mom, Sharon, asked us to pick four
words to base our marriage on and four Bible verses to correlate with each word. She
wanted to make a plaque for the cornerstones of our marriage. We sat down to pick out
our words with all the delusion and anticipation of bright-eyed newlyweds, our hands
clasped tightly in bliss. Here is what we came up with:

FAITHFULNESS:

We will always be loyal and faithful to one another. There would never be any dishonesty or betrayal.

> "Be faithful, even to the point of death, and I will give you life as your victor's crown" (Revelation 2:10b).

JOY:

We were going to have fun and laugh no matter what.

> "Yet I will rejoice in the LORD, I will be joyful in God my Savior" (Habakkuk 3:18).

CONTENTMENT:

We would be happy with simplicity, especially as we entered into a career in ministry.

> "I know what it is to be in need, and I know what it is to have plenty. I have learned the secret of being content in any and every situation, whether well-fed or hungry, whether living in plenty or want. I can do all this through him, who gives me strength" (Philippians 4:12-13).

SERVANTHOOD:

Knowing what ministry would take, we wanted to embody servanthood to each other and our future children.

> "In your relationships with one another, have the same mindset as Christ Jesus: Who, being in very nature God, did not consider equality with God something to be used to his own advantage; rather, he made himself nothing by taking the very nature of a servant, being made in human likeness" (Philippians 2:5-7).

We proudly displayed our list to Sharon, faces beaming. After reviewing the list, she said, "These are good, but what about love?"

Love? We shrugged. *Well, that was a given.* In our eagerness to plan our perfect future, we overlooked the one necessary thing to survive a marriage: love.

NOISY GONG AND CLANGING CYMBALS

Almost all newly engaged couples fit the following criteria:

* They are emotionally passionate.

* They have a lot to learn.

If the apostle Paul had sat with us that day as we plotted our marriage foundations, he would have agreed with my mother-in-law. In 1 Corinthians, he wrote about the uselessness of having accomplishments and strong character traits without love. Read what he wrote in the opening sentences of chapter 13.

> **If I speak in the tongues of men and of angels but have not love, I am a noisy gong or a clanging cymbal. And if I have prophetic powers, and understand all mysteries and all knowledge, and if I have all faith, so as to remove mountains, but have not love, I am nothing. If I give away all I have, and if I deliver up my body to be burned but have not love, I gain nothing (1 Corinthians 13:1-3).**

We weren't the only ones missing love. The audience of this letter was a new church in Corinth. If you read the rest of Paul's letter to them, you will notice they are much like a newly engaged couple.

They were emotionally passionate. They were easily swayed by different leaders, quick to choose favorites, eager to practice spiritual gifts and communion even if they didn't understand it, and prone to make haste decisions.

They had a lot to learn. They missed the big picture of how to treat each other and had to work to become knowledgeable about using their diversity and spiritual gifts to work together.

Just like Zach and I as newlyweds, the church members in Corinth had lofty goals but lacked a solid foundational base. Again, their intentions were strong:

* speak in tongues

* have prophetic powers

* understand mysteries and knowledge

* have faith to move mountains

* give away all they have to the point of martyrdom

Wow! Talk about some great things to add to your cart. They were high on emotion and ready to go. The problem was just doing good things without love underneath it all doesn't have staying power. Soon, you will lose motivation, and the high will fizzle out. It's impossible to sustain.

Impossible is where God does his best work.

THE BAR: IMPOSSIBLE

After establishing that love is the most important thing, Paul lists what love is and isn't.

> **Love is patient, love is kind. It does not envy, it does not boast, it is not proud. It does not dishonor others, it is not self-seeking, it is not easily**

angered, it keeps no record of wrongs. Love does not delight in evil but rejoices with the truth. It always protects, always trusts, always hopes, always perseveres. Love never fails (1 Corinthians 13:4-8a).

Paul uses eight words to describe what love is and eight words to describe what love isn't. This list is enough to make even a madly-in-love engaged couple deflate like an untied balloon.

LOVE IS:

1) patient

2) kind

3) rejoices with the truth

4) bears all things

5) believes all things

6) hopes all things

7) endures all things

8) never ends

LOVE IS NOT:

1) envious

2) boastful

3) arrogant

4) rude

5) self-seeking

6) irritable

7) resentful

8) delighting in evil

If this is the standard, it's pretty depressing. What marriage, relationship, church, or community can last if this is the standard? The answer is none.

FULLY KNOWN

In the last section of chapter 13, Paul explains why, even if we start with a boost of adrenaline and take off in a fit of passion, it won't last. Those things are short-lived. Mountaintop moments pass. Spiritual high moments are fantastic but insufficient to build a forever relationship. Even gifts of the Spirit can fade away.

But where there are prophecies, they will cease; where there are tongues, they will be stilled; where there is knowledge, it will pass away.

For we know in part and we prophesy in part, but when completeness comes, what is in part disappears. When I was a child, I talked like a child, I thought like a child, I reasoned like a child. When I became a man, I put the ways of childhood behind me. For now we see only a reflection as in a mirror; then we shall see face to face. Now I know in part; then I shall know fully, even as I am fully known. (1 Corinthians 13:8b-12)

Paul reminded this young, little, passionate church that maturity will come, just like a child growing up or like a marriage going through the school of hard knocks. So, what hope do we have of adding love to our cart if the bar for true love is impossible?

"But when completeness comes."

What completeness are we talking about here? That thing definitely can't be you or me. It has to be Jesus. **When Jesus came, he brought salvation to the whole world.**

The salvation Paul describes is access to a level of intimacy we all want. It's a face-to-face, fully known kind of love, the right kind to add to your cart. Isn't that what every newly engaged couple desires? To be seen just as we are with no mask and still loved?

Sharon kept the four cornerstones we picked that day, but thankfully, she added a fifth foundational base to the plaque still displayed in our living room. The word she added, of course, was LOVE at the bottom of the plaque. It holds up all the other wonderful attributes we still strive for today. The Scripture she chose from the Bible was the fitting words of Paul in 1 Corinthians 13.

"Love is patient, love is kind. It does not envy, it does not boast, it is not proud...It always protects, always trusts, always hopes, always perseveres. Love never fails" (1 Corinthians 13:4,7-8).

UNBOX YOUR LOVE TODAY.

ZEHNDER FAMILY CORNERSTONES

FAITHFULNESS
"Be FAITHFUL, even to the point of death, and I will give you the crown of life."
Revelation 2:10

JOY
"Yet I will rejoice in the Lord, I will be JOYFUL in God my Savior."
Habakkuk 3:18

CONTENTMENT
"I know what it is to be in need, and I know what it is to have plenty. I have learned the secret of being CONTENT in any and every situation... I can do all things through Him who gives me strength."
Philippians 4:12-13

SERVANTHOOD
"Your attitude should be the same as that of Christ Jesus: who, being in very nature God, did not consider equality with God something to be grasped, but made Himself nothing, taking the very nature of a SERVANT."
Philippians 2:5-7

FOUNDATIONAL BASE: **LOVE**
"We LOVE because He first loved us."
1 John 4:19

"LOVE is patient, LOVE is kind. It does not envy, it does not boast, it is not proud ... It always protects, always trusts, always hopes, always perseveres. LOVE never fails."
1 Corinthians 13:4, 7-8

CHALLENGE DAY 20
JOY: ADD TO CART

Write down the top five things that bring you love.

1 _____

2 _____

3 _____

4 _____

5 _____

While there are many ways that God gives love to you, it's important to remember that all love ultimately comes from God. He should always be at the top of the list. Go to **www.redletterchallenge.com/adventverses** and read the ten Bible verses on love. Write down and memorize one of the Bible verses as you unbox love.

DAY 21

LOVE:

CHECKOUT

"SEE WHAT GREAT LOVE THE FATHER HAS LAVISHED ON US, THAT WE SHOULD BE CALLED CHILDREN OF GOD!" (1 JOHN 3:1A).

CAN YOU HEAR ME NOW?

As humans, we understand that love has a cost. But what's the limit? The debt of sin is beyond what any mind can comprehend. Today, you will read about this unlimited, unfathomable love Jesus purchased for you.

The first cell phone Zach and I got was a 2002 entry-level Nokia. We got the phones for free when signing a year-long contract for $35 a month. What a feeling! Anyone could reach us anywhere! We felt so high-tech and free. But we soon discovered there were some parameters. We could only send limited texts and had a certain number of monthly minutes to talk. At the end of the billing cycle, when we would receive a call, we would have to call them back on a landline to save our minutes!

A few years later, our contract changed, and the best thing happened: We no longer had to count minutes because we were put on AT&T's *Unlimited and More* plan. We soon found out, however, that AT&T had two unlimited plans: *Unlimited and More* and *Unlimited and More Premium.* (That should have been our first clue that something was a little amiss. How can you have something *more* than unlimited?)

Since we were early customers, AT&T grandfathered us into their "unlimited" data plan. Even though we were paying a higher-than-average bill, we got all the data we wanted and never could go over. No more counting minutes!

Eventually, however, we learned what "unlimited" meant to AT&T. Once we had used up a certain amount of data, our phone company would still allow us to use our phones, but there was a catch. The speed slowed to a trickle. Throttling slows down data after a certain threshold, and we felt cheated. Once we realized that our "unlimited" minutes were minimal, we went back to counting our minutes.

"What good is it to be grandfathered into a plan?" Zach questioned the poor customer service rep on the phone. "I'm paying more, yet my phone is slower than everyone else!"

The U.S.A. was one of many countries needing help with its unlimited promises. For example, in the UK, providers can no longer use the term "unlimited" according to The Fair Usage Policy (FUP), a set of guidelines established by mobile carriers to ensure equitable usage of their network resources. Zach and I discovered that there is no such thing as unlimited. Everything has its limit—everything, that is, except God.

UNLIMITED LOVE

There are no limits on God and his love. Below are three ways that God is unlimited:

* God's original love is unlimited.

* His sacrifice is unlimited.

* The reach of that love is unlimited.

THERE ARE NO LIMITS ON GOD AND HIS LOVE.

First of all, God is unlimited love. Because God is triune, three-in-one, love existed before humanity. Remember, Jesus was around way before he came as a baby. Genesis uses a plural article for the Hebrew word *Elohim* to describe the first time God was mentioned. **"In the beginning, Elohim created the heaven and earth" (Genesis 1:1, NOG).**

The plural article doesn't mean there are multiple gods. There is only one God. But all three persons of the Trinity were present at creation. They had always existed, exchanging love with one another. So, God didn't need to wait for us to have love already in existence. Love has always been and always will be. Jesus talks about this togetherness in the verse below.

> **"On that day you will realize that I am in my Father, and you are in me, and I am in you" (John 14:20).**

Second, Jesus Christ was God's unlimited gift to the world. It was already incredible that he humbled himself as a baby. There is no way the enemy could have predicted Jesus's death. God did not limit his gift but sacrificed himself on the cross. No other religion on earth has God coming to earth, humiliating himself by taking on all the sins of others. They have gods that give good gifts or gods that can do mighty acts of power. But they wouldn't go so far as to die.

> **"He is the atoning sacrifice for our sins: and not for ours only, but also for the sins of the whole world" (1 John 2:2).**

Lastly, the Bible says Jesus died for every person. God's Christmas gift is unlimited. There are no stipulations, secret clauses, or throttling. God's love isn't contingent on your good behavior. It's fast and free for all. In the last invitation found in the Bible, our Lord opens the door as wide as he can by saying,

"The Spirit and the bride say, 'Come!' And let the one who hears say, 'Come!' Let the one who is thirsty come; and let the one who wishes take the free gift of the water of life" (Revelation 22:17).

A FLOOD OF LOVE

As you examine this gift of love today, you will learn that it is unlimited in its origin, sacrifice, and reach. But the cost is unfathomable. We just can't afford it. The good news is that you don't have to.

"See what great love the Father has lavished on us, that we should be called children of God! And that is what we are! The reason the world does not know us is that it did not know him" (1 John 3:1).

The NIV translates the Greek word *didomi,* which means "given," as lavish. Lavish is bestowing something generously or extravagantly. The word comes from the old French *lavas,* which means 'great flood of rain.' What a cool picture!

God's love is a flood of rain all over you. To understand how powerful this image is, you have to know the history of what people thought about water.

Water was not originally a sign of love to the ancient people. Water meant chaos. Remember how Genesis started?

"Now the earth was formless and empty, darkness was over the surface of the deep, and the Spirit of God was hovering over the waters" (Genesis 1:2).

If those waters meant the absence of God or total chaos and disorder, then the act of creation was bringing order to creation. Later on, water was still treated as evil because when God judged the people, it came as a flood. After that event, water continued to mean punishment. If God said he was sending water, people ran in fear. *Don't send water, Lord! That will kill us! We can't stand it.*

But God reversed the idea of water as a punishment to make water a cleansing, saving act. It all began when he parted the waters in the book of Exodus. Waters didn't kill the Israelites. God made water the way to their salvation. After that, washing and water got a whole new meaning. It was a way to freedom.

Water now brings newness. In your baptism, water is not a means of killing but bringing life. Rejoice in the flood of love rain today. It was purchased with the price of Jesus's body and blood. He paid that impossible price for you through the cross, and now God calls you children of God. Hit that "Buy it Now" button and receive that unlimited love gift.

Don't worry about the cost. Jesus has it covered, and your minutes are unlimited!

UNBOX YOUR LOVE TODAY.

CHALLENGE DAY 21
LOVE CHECKOUT

Water is a part of your daily life. Without water, you wouldn't last long. Each time you use water today, think about and thank God for the miracle he performed at your baptism and the price he paid to soak you with his love.

OPTIONAL CHALLENGE

If you've never been baptized, talk to your local church leaders about how to get baptized. If you get baptized, please let us know at **hello@redletterchallenge.com** so we can encourage you. And make sure to include **#RedLetterAdvent** on any baptism pictures you may share with others.

DAY 22 ♡

LOVE:

IN TRANSIT

"FOR IT IS BY GRACE YOU HAVE BEEN SAVED, THROUGH FAITH—AND THIS IS NOT FROM YOURSELVES, IT IS THE GIFT OF GOD— NOT BY WORKS, SO THAT NO ONE CAN BOAST" (EPHESIANS 2:8-9)

NO STRINGS ATTACHED

God has already displayed his love, and yet we are still waiting for that love to be fully realized when he returns. While we wait, during the In Transit Stage, it's tempting to sit back and think God's taking care of it all. But while love is entirely free and God is ultimately in control, it doesn't mean your choices and actions don't matter.

Have you ever heard the phrase, "There's no such thing as a free lunch?" If that's true, then why do I always fall for that "free" stuff? Too often, I'll sign up for free trials to sample something and then forget to cancel and end up paying a lot for something I don't even use. The offer of "free" comes back to bite me. This plays out in other parts of my life.

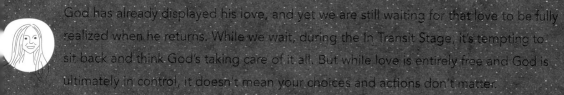

Holidays are not always loving and happy times for people. While there may be a price to pay for an expensive gift, God's gift has no strings attached. As the verse says below, salvation is entirely based on grace.

"FOR IT IS BY GRACE YOU HAVE BEEN SAVED, THROUGH FAITH—AND THIS IS NOT FROM YOURSELVES, IT IS THE GIFT OF GOD— NOT BY WORKS, SO THAT NO ONE CAN BOAST" (EPHESIANS 2:8-9).

You had nothing to do with your salvation. If a gift is earned or deserved, it is no longer a gift. It's a paycheck or earned bonus. But this gift was 100% free.

Regarding those who work to earn their way into heaven, Jesus said,

> "Many will say to me on that day, 'Lord, Lord, did we not prophesy in your name and in your name drive out demons and in your name perform many miracles?' Then I will tell them plainly, 'I never knew you. Away from me, you evildoers!'" (Matthew 7:22-23).

These attempts to earn salvation are called "works of iniquity." No matter how good those works may be, they are still something you do with a string attached. If someone could earn heaven, then the motive would be selfish. Jesus was entirely motivated by love.

While we are in wait mode, it's easy to want to leave it all to God, but his plan involves you. Your actions have more influence than you thought, but it's hard to grasp this paradox.

A PUPPET ON STRINGS

Some people believe everything if life is already set, and it doesn't matter what you do. God will have his way. Fate will happen in the end. So, in other words, we are like puppets on a string. Our choices don't matter. God's will will be done in the end. You might see this in inspirational stoic quotes about accepting everything that happens without being ruffled.

Other people believe the opposite. They think you hold the steering wheel of life, and it's up to you to make or break your future. In this picture, we are like a ship lost at sea, trying to navigate independently with a distant God watching from above. You might see examples of this in movies where the hero has to save the day. It's all up to him.

So, which is it? It's both.

God is absolutely in control over everything, and still, your choices matter and have consequences. This is a paradox. It might seem absurd and untrue until you read the Bible and see it is exactly what it says. We have to accept both of these truths at once.

This is good news for us because we want to have purpose and meaning. I want to know that what I do matters, but I also love that I don't have to carry the weight of responsibility for how everything turns out. If that were the case, I would never leave the house!

God's riches are given to you, not with strings attached, but with a grace-filled purpose.

G.R.A.C.E.

Everything you have, you got one of three ways: you earned it, stole it, or somebody gave it to you. Which of these does grace fall under?

Earn it. Could we earn heaven? If we had a million lifetimes and worked day and night, there is no way we could. Only absolute purity can exist in God's presence. Not one person, outside of Jesus, could ever make the claim to be perfect. There is no way we could earn heaven. So that's out.

Stole It. Heaven isn't something we can sneak into or steal. There isn't someone at the pearly gates checking your ticket.

Given it. If we can't earn or steal it, then there is only one other way to enjoy heaven: it must be a gift. And that is precisely what the Bible says.

A helpful acrostic to remember is **G.R.A.C.E.**

GOD'S
RICHES
AT
CHRIST'S
EXPENSE

Tim Keller reminds us that this God is unique in his ability to enter your suffering.

> **If God really has been born in a manger, then we have something that no other religion even claims to have. It's a God who truly understands you from the inside of your experience. There's no other religion that says God has suffered, that God had to be courageous, that he knows what it's like to be abandoned by friends, to be crushed by injustice, to be tortured and die. Christmas shows he knows what you are going through. When you talk to him, he understands.**[33]

You have a wonderful gift, but it comes at a cost. When we try to earn our salvation, it can feel like a burden rather than a gift. Its cost is too great. Jesus gives you this beautiful gift and doesn't make you carry the load. That's great news for you!

There may still be no such thing as a free lunch, but the gift of eternal life has been won and is available to you free of charge!

UNBOX YOUR LOVE TODAY.

CHALLENGE DAY 22
LOVE: IN TRANSIT

While you wait in transit, you have a calling to serve others. Show love by buying a coffee or lunch for someone today, with no strings attached. After all, there may be such a thing as a free lunch (for someone else)!

DAY 23

LOVE:

HANDLE
WITH CARE

"AS I HAVE LOVED YOU, SO YOU MUST LOVE ONE ANOTHER. BY THIS EVERYONE WILL KNOW THAT YOU ARE MY DISCIPLES, IF YOU LOVE ONE ANOTHER" (JOHN 13:34B-35).

IN-APP PURCHASES

Although Christmas brings joyful anticipation, you still live in a world filled with pain. For some, the broken parts of this world overshadow the season. We need to remember to handle those people with care and concern. Today in Love: Handle with Care, you will reflect on how we search for the love we already have in our possession.

One year, I got a new iPad, but many of my purchased apps were no longer showing up as owned, so I had to repurchase them. Is there anything more frustrating than buying what you already have?

I felt robbed and cheated when something I bought would not show as mine. I refused to spend money on something I already owned. That made no sense! After calling customer service, we discovered a glitch in the system, and all my purchased apps were downloaded free of charge. Who would spend money on something they already own?

THE FOUND TREASURE

Businessman and art dealer William Randolph Hearst was almost guilty of that very thing. Hearst was a collector of international art and spent a great deal of time and money collecting art. One day, he found a description of a painting he just had to have. So, he sent his art agent on a worldwide search to find it. After months of searching, the agent discovered the treasure.

I imagine the conversation going something like this:

> **Agent:** Sir, I am happy to report that I have discovered the whereabouts of your desired artwork.

> **Hearst:** Wonderful! I knew you could do it.

> **Agent:** Happy to serve you, milord.

> **Hearst:** Well then, what's the damage? This will set me back quite a pretty penny.

> **Agent:** Indeed, the artwork is very expensive. But it won't cost you a dime.

> **Hearst:** What do you mean? Have you stolen it? Good heavens! I never intended for that!

> **Agent:** No, no. I didn't steal it—the artwork is in a warehouse owned by William Randolph Hearst.

> **Hearst:** Now that's a cruel joke, sir. What kind of trick are you trying to pull? I don't find this very funny.

Agent: Sir, I'm not playing a joke. You already own it. It is located in your warehouse, never uncrated, and is safe and sound.

Written in *Illustrations for Biblical Preaching* by Michael Green, this story shows what can happen when we can't keep track of all we own because we have so much.[34] This true story may sound absurd to you. After all, who would spend thousands, or even millions, on a piece of artwork they already owned? You may not be an art dealer, but I bet there have been times when you have found yourself in the same boat. We have all spent money getting more of what we already have.

EVERYBODY'S LOOKING FOR LOVE

Love is what people are searching for.

The Beatles, a famous music band, sang, "All you need is love."

Writer Amantine de Francueil, known by her pen name George Sand, wrote, "There is only one happiness in this life, to love and be loved."

Aristotle was a famous Greek philosopher whose ideas shaped our world today. He also commented on love: "Love is composed of a single soul inhabiting two bodies."

The apostle John, one of Jesus's disciples, wrote the book of 1 John. He was older when he wrote this letter to a group of house churches in crisis in Ephesus. The comforting words he offered were all about love.

> **"This is how God showed his love among us: He sent his one and only Son into the world that we might live through him. This is love: not that we loved God, but that he loved us and sent his Son as an atoning sacrifice for our sins. Dear friends, since God so loved us, we also ought to love one another" (1 John 4:9-11).**

I love *Strong's* definition of love in the first verse. The literal translation is "love feast." Re-read the verse below with the literal translation replacing love.

"This is how God's love feast was made clear among us."

The love God demonstrates to you is a feast. Why?

A bunch of people will share it. There will be more than enough. It is something to celebrate.

This is a fantastic promise personally for me to hear right before we celebrate Christmas. Zach and I both grew up in ministry families. Now that we are in ministry, our Christmas Eve consists of many church services, just like when we were growing up. Zach usually preaches, and the boys and I volunteer. So, our Christmas Eve dinner is Chinese takeout or frozen pizza late at night. It's encouraging to hear that God's love is a feast waiting for us!

More love was offered to us than we could ever consume. God doesn't just prepare the table; he also brings us the invitation. He handles you with care. He doesn't make you find his love. It's already in your possession. How sad would that be if you missed God's love like Hearst missed the artwork sitting in his warehouse!

God sent his one and only Son into the world. Ultimate love was not the pitiful and inconsistent love we show one another, but Jesus's atoning sacrifice for our sins. Now, this love is sitting in the warehouse of your soul. The question is, are you opening it? Or are you falling for a counterfeit love?

THE TRAGIC ENDING

Out of the top fifty romance movies, only two end happily ever after. If love is what we are after, why can't it last for two hours in a film? *Gone with the Wind*, *Titanic*,

Casablanca, Romeo and Juliet, La La Land, The Notebook, Ghost, and *A Star is Born* are all examples of movies with tragic endings.

There is a reason that romantic love does not usually end well in movies. The only way to keep that fever-heat fervor is to leave it unfulfilled. The moment you get it, that fever-love begins to disappear. It just has no staying power, like a forgery for the real love of God.

God's love story is way better than any human love story. **You are so loved and desired.** Not only is he the lover of your soul, but he will handle you with care.

But wait! You say. *There can't be a death in an ultimate love story. Death means no more love.*

That is the shocking surprise of the gospel. There was love after death. Your movie didn't end when the credits rolled.

When the credits rolled for Jesus, the stone rolled, too.

You are living after the movie. Jesus's love story included tragic separation, just like all the romantic movies. But it didn't end with that death.

Jesus stood up and walked out. Love came back and freed us from captivity. You don't have to live in fear that your love will end. **Your love story has a happily ever after!**

Ripping this gift of love open is the best thing you can do with it! Jesus said,

> **"As I have loved you, so you must love one another. By this everyone will know that you are my disciples, if you love one another" (John 13:34b-35).**

We must handle famous artwork carefully, but love is a gift to be opened, enjoyed, and shared. William Randolph Hearst owned the coveted art but couldn't keep it. During the

Great Depression, he sold all his art to pay off enormous debts and died without owning any of his masterpieces.

Hearst may have had to give up his treasures, but you never will. God's love is in your possession now and always will be. You don't have to search for it or pay for it. **God's love is your masterpiece forever**.

UNBOX YOUR LOVE TODAY.

CHALLENGE DAY 23
LOVE: HANDLE WITH CARE

Some of the hardest working people in this season are those who literally deliver all of your "handle with care" packages. Today, give away the love of Jesus by writing a "thank you" note to your mail carrier or delivery person. If you can, include a gift card or financial gift to bless them in this season. Please note, USPS workers are not able to accept a cash gift of $20 or more.

DAY 24 ♡

LOVE:

DELIVERED

"AND NOW THESE THREE REMAIN: FAITH, HOPE, AND LOVE. BUT THE GREATEST OF THESE IS LOVE" (1 CORINTHIANS 13:13).

THANKSGIVING ON CHRISTMAS EVE?

Love has arrived. Christmas Eve is here! The gifts of hope, peace, joy, and love are available to you. These presents aren't fads or trendy; they are gifts God wants you to open and experience.

One of the most incredible ways God delivers his love is through his provision. In the hustle and bustle of life, especially in Advent, it can be natural to plow through our days without practicing gratitude. But, on Christmas Eve morning, I've found a great opportunity to practice gratitude.

The night before, Allison and I will gather all the gifts hidden in closets, drawers, nooks, crannies, and everywhere else we've tried to outsmart our kids from finding them. Then, we will place all the gifts underneath the tree for the morning's big reveal so that when the kids wake up, they are excited!

But, before they wake up, there is a moment that I've found to be one of the most meaningful in the entire Advent season. Looking at what's underneath the tree, I find myself overwhelmed by God's provision. God reminds me he has been faithful. He's not only given us what we need, but as I look at all of the gifts underneath the tree, I see he's also given us many things we want. As a parent beams with pride when their kids open gifts, I imagine God doing the same in heaven as we bask in this provision. After all, it was Jesus that reminded us of this truth.

"IF YOU, THEN, THOUGH YOU ARE EVIL, KNOW HOW TO GIVE GOOD GIFTS TO YOUR CHILDREN, HOW MUCH MORE WILL YOUR FATHER IN HEAVEN GIVE GOOD GIFTS TO THOSE WHO ASK HIM!" (MATTHEW 7:11).

We have a God who loves to give us good gifts. As we prepare to open Christmas gifts in the next couple of days, let us remember to be grateful for a God who not only delivered the greatest gift of all, Jesus, but who continues to give us good gifts.

As you read about good gifts from the past, you may recall the excitement you experienced when you opened them as a kid.

CHRISTMAS GIFTS OF THE PAST

The most popular Christmas gifts in America have changed dramatically. In the early 1900s, Christmas was simple. Never mind what was under the tree; only one in five had a Christmas tree in those years! If you did have a tree, and there was a present under that tree, the greatest gifts you could expect to receive were a pack of Crayola crayons, a rocking horse, oranges, and nuts.

I'm trying to imagine my boys' reaction if they had received oranges and crayons for Christmas when they were younger. I doubt they would have been impressed.

Okay, Mom and Dad, that's funny. Where are the real gifts?!?

Things only improved a little in the following decade. The gifts of the 1910s were gloves, mittens, and handkerchiefs. Warm hands and a clean, wiped chin were all one could hope for at the beginning of the century. Christmas gifts improved a bit in the 1920s when the gift of the decade was actually a toy: the Yo-Yo. Then, the 1930s introduced us to classic toys still around today: the Red Ryder wagon and BB Guns.

Perhaps looking for a softer and…er…less dangerous toy, the 1940s toy of the decade was the Bubble solution. Maybe everyone was still recovering from the BBs of the past. Then we get to the second half of the 20th century.

In the 1950s, the Hula Hoop, Pez Dispensers, and LEGO made the list for the first time. The Etch-a-Sketch and LEGO ignited creativity, along with GI Joes in the 1960s. In the 1970s, Star Wars action figures came around, a game called Pong, and LEGO continued to dominate the charts for the third straight decade. But the #1 gift of the decade just 40 years ago was a Rock in a Box. Yes, the Pet Rock made over 15 million dollars.[35] Maybe we were yearning for the simpler days? Wildly, people went along with it.

The 1980s gift of the decade was called the "My Buddy" doll. Video games sprung on the scene in the 1990s with Nintendo. Power Rangers, Super Soakers water guns, and the Tickle Me Elmo doll were also desired gifts. To help propel them into the 21st century, kids asked for Razor Scooters, the latest Nintendo Wii, PlayStation 2, Elmo Live, and still LEGO in the 2000s. (Maybe the only timeless and changeless things in this world are Jesus and LEGO!)

Finally, the toys of the decade for the 2010s were more video games and electronics, plus Elsa dolls and Hatchimals. Gifts have changed significantly over the past 100+ years, but there has always been one constant gift: Jesus.

THE CONSTANT GIFT

Most of the Christmas gifts delivered several years ago have disappeared in memory. Can you even name what you got for Christmas last year? What about two years ago? Three? Unlike those brightly wrapped packages that took hours to shop and wrap, minutes to open, and later forgotten, Jesus is always current and never changes. He is the same today to those who trust him as he was to those two thousand years ago. As we are now waiting for Jesus to return, we can trust in the unchanging love of Jesus.

Times, styles, attitudes, and tastes change, but Jesus Christ is God's unchanging gift delivered to you. On Day 20, you explored the whole chapter of 1 Corinthians 13, except for verse thirteen. Let's look at it now.

"AND NOW THESE THREE REMAIN: FAITH, HOPE, AND LOVE. BUT THE GREATEST OF THESE IS LOVE" (1 CORINTHIANS 13:13).

Love is the most important of all God's gifts. But aren't things like hope and faith important? How can love be the greatest? To understand why love is the greatest, we must return to the beginning.

LOVE IS
THE MOST
IMPORTANT
OF ALL
GOD'S GIFTS.

In the Garden of Eden, love was perfect between God and us.

> **"So God created mankind in his own image, in the image of God he created them; male and female he created them. God blessed them and said to them, 'Be fruitful and increase in number; fill the earth and subdue it'" (Genesis 1:27-28a).**

Adam and Eve didn't need faith and hope in the Garden of Eden because they had perfect love with God. They saw him, so they didn't need faith. They were in a right relationship with him, so they didn't need hope. But that all ended when they left the garden.

YESTERDAY, TODAY, AND FOREVER

You and I need faith and hope because we can no longer access God as Adam and Eve did. Sin is blocking us from God. But you can have faith that God is real and a rope hope that one day you will be in a right relationship with him again in heaven.

Someday, everything will be as it should be. When you see God face to face, you will no longer need faith in him. Love will absorb faith. When you are in Heaven, you won't need hope anymore. You will be where you have always wanted to be. Love will absorb hope. So, without faith and hope, only one thing is left—love. Love will always remain.

"JESUS CHRIST IS THE SAME YESTERDAY AND TODAY AND FOREVER" (HEBREWS 13:8).

Oranges and nuts will get eaten. Wagons rust, dolls lose their hair, and video games become obsolete. **Jesus's love for you will always be your greatest gift.**

UNBOX YOUR LOVE TODAY.

CHALLENGE DAY 24
LOVE: DELIVERED

Prayer Time. Before opening your gifts today or tomorrow, say a prayer thanking God for his provision, both for your needs and your wants. If you have a family, lead your family in this prayer time. Finally, after opening your gifts, get in the Christmas spirit by delivering a gift to someone less fortunate.

DAY 25 ♡

LOVE:

RETURNS

"I WILL RESCUE YOU FROM YOUR OWN PEOPLE AND FROM THE GENTILES. I AM SENDING YOU TO THEM TO OPEN THEIR EYES AND TURN THEM FROM DARKNESS TO LIGHT" (ACTS 26:17-18A).

MANY HAPPY RETURNS

Merry Christmas! If you lived across the pond in England and wished someone a Merry Christmas, a typical response would be "And many happy returns to you!" or "Many happy returns of the day!"

This does not mean they hope you will return many of your gifts after you open them. That would be a rude response. Returns are not happy; they are annoying!

When the British say returns, they mean yield or profit, like *investment returns*. In this sense, a return is how much extra an investor makes from their initial yearly investment. It's often shown as a percentage. So, like an investment return, "Many happy returns of the day" simply means wishing that someone's initial happiness would multiply and grow.

The title for today, Love: Returns, isn't about returning that love to the giver. **The love return is when we multiply the love given to us by giving it away to others.** What does the Bible say about multiplying or growing love?

THE INITIAL INVESTMENT

You have learned that God's investment to love you was huge. More than faith or hope, love is the most important thing and will last forever. The price of love was beyond what we could ever pay, so God came down and died in our place. It was the greatest act of love the world has ever known. Because of that, we now have the gift of love with no strings attached. But often, we confuse our longing for God's love with the counterfeit love of this world. Those fake forgeries deceive us into looking for love in other places. Despite our faithlessness, God's love is strong and faithful. He refuses to give up on his people and keeps placing his love back into our hands.

So, what are we doing with this unearned treasure of love?

In the Scripture below, God showed Paul the tremendous lengths he would go to give him this precious gift. Read about what crazy thing God did to Paul while he was traveling to a city called Damascus. (Back then, people called him Saul.)

> **On one of these journeys I was going to Damascus with the authority and commission of the chief priests. About noon, King Agrippa, as I was on the road, I saw a light from Heaven, brighter than the sun, blazing around me and my companions. We all fell to the ground, and I heard a voice saying to me in Aramaic "Saul, Saul, why do you persecute me? It is hard for you to kick against the goads." Then I asked, "Who are you, Lord?" (Acts 26:12-15a)**

Right at lunchtime, a bright light appeared to Saul. It blinded Saul for weeks. The light was God himself.

After blindsiding him, God spoke to Saul. Rather than yelling at him for persecuting Christians, God asked why Saul was persecuting him. Saul was in shock. He didn't know how he was hurting God. He thought he was doing a good thing by stopping the Christians. All Saul could ask was who that light was. God answered him and gave him directions on what he should do next. Continue reading about what God told Saul to do.

> 'I am Jesus, whom you are persecuting,' the Lord replied. 'Now get up
> and stand on your feet. I have appeared to you to appoint you as a
> servant and as a witness of what you have seen and will see of me. I will
> rescue you from your people and from the Gentiles. I am sending you to
> them to open their eyes and turn them from darkness to light, and from
> the power of Satan to God, so that they may receive forgiveness of sins
> and a place among those sanctified by faith in me.' (Acts 26:15b-18)

God wasn't just interested in getting Saul to believe he was real or having a relationship with him. Those are important and necessary things. You have to believe in God through faith that he gives, and you have to spend time with God. But here's the thing: if belief were all God was after, he would have taken Saul into Heaven then and there. Instead, Jesus changed his name, from Saul to Paul, and changed his life. He said,

> "I want you to be my spokesperson. I'm sending you off to tell people
> that their sins are forgiven and because of that, you get to tell them
> they have a place in the family. You get to invite them into the company
> of those who begin real living by believing in me."

God challenged Paul. He responded, "Many happy returns on this love I am giving you, Paul!"

Before this encounter, Paul opposed God's work. If God can pick someone like Paul to be a powerful spokesperson, what stops him from choosing someone like me or you? Nothing! There's a beautiful calling in your life beyond just assuring you have a place in Heaven. And it had nothing to do with your actions. You could not save yourself or choose yourself for this task. All that work belongs to God.

> **"You did not choose me, but I chose you and appointed you so that you might go and bear fruit—fruit that will last—and so that whatever you ask in my name the Father will give you" (John 15:16).**

The most selfish thing we can do is open this gift of love that Jesus so freely delivers and keep it for ourselves. Instead, God calls us to share it with others and show them who Jesus is. So, how are we doing? Let's ask an atheist.

LETTING THE LOVE OUT

Not everyone wants to hear about Jesus. Many people range from an amused response to outright anger when you bring up Jesus.

Penn Jillette, the famous magician and atheist, has a different opinion about Christians than most atheists. Read his take below.

> I've always said I don't respect people who don't proselytize. I don't respect that at all. If you believe that there's a heaven and a hell, and people could be going to hell or not getting eternal life, and you think that it's not really worth telling them this because it would make it socially awkward—and atheists who think people shouldn't proselytize and who say leave me alone and keep your religion to yourself—how much do you have to hate somebody not to proselytize? How much do you have to hate somebody to believe everlasting life is possible and not tell them that? I mean, if I believed, beyond the shadow of a doubt, that a truck was coming at you,

and you didn't believe that truck was bearing down on you, there is a certain point where I tackle you. And this is more important than that.

This is sad because Jillette is right. If we believe that people's salvation is in the balance, why aren't we telling everyone we know about Jesus? Paul got a wake-up call, and he used it. He took that love investment and had many happy returns on it. Read what he wrote to the church of Philippi.

> **"I'm not saying that I have this all together, that I have it made. But I am well on my way, reaching out for Christ, who has so wondrously reached out for me" (Philippians 3:12, MSG).**

Those happy returns drove Paul to pursue everyone, even to being called crazy! Read the last verse for today below. It's a good one to go out on.

> **"If we are 'out of our mind,' as some say, it is for God; if we are in our right mind, it is for you. For Christ's love compels us, because we are convinced that one died for all, and therefore all died" (2 Corinthians 5:13-14).**

What motivates you to go out and be so bold about Jesus that people might think you are a little nuts?! It's the grace of Jesus! You don't share because you feel guilty or obligated. You spread his gospel and pursue God's lost children because Christ's love motivates you. **You don't just want to tell people about Jesus; you must!** After all that he's done for you, you can't keep it inside any longer.

So, Merry Christmas, and I pray you have many happy returns of God's love.

UNBOX YOUR LOVE TODAY.

CHALLENGE DAY 25
LOVE: RETURNS

While giving away gifts is an essential part of the Christmas season, there is no more excellent gift to return than the gift of Jesus. As you celebrate the birth of Jesus today, think of those in your life with whom you can share the Good News of Jesus over the coming year. Commit to praying for each of them by name and seeking opportunities in the near future to share how Jesus has made a difference in your life.

ACKNOWLEDGMENTS

Advent has been a practice in my life since I was a child. Its rhythms are as much a part of Christmas for me as anything else. I'd like to express my heartfelt gratitude to my parents, Roger and Alice Buck, for instilling these beautiful traditions into my life. Your love and guidance have shaped me for the better.

We pitched the idea of *Red Letter Advent* to our team in February 2024. Despite knowing it would be a quick turnaround and tight timeline, we received the same response: positivity, enthusiasm, and unwavering support. Thank you, Steven and Susan Blount, for your faithful service, Anne McLaughlin, for your excellent attention to detail, and Brenda and David, for your hard work and dedication. Also, thanks to Kayla Marty, Pastor Jacob Baumann, Sharon Zehnder, Dan Hoppen, and Brenda Sanders for your editing help.

Unboxed was a sermon series originally preached at theCross in Mt. Dora, FL, in Advent of 2019 and 2020. We thank Mark, Jacob, Chris, and the team at theCross for their contribution in brainstorming and crafting this concept.

Finally, huge thanks to Zach for the opportunity to work on this project together. Writing a book is like having a child. A draft is demanding, uncooperative, and inconvenient. There are intense work hours and pushing to deadlines. But the joy and relief of seeing this project come into the world is a feeling like no other. ZZ, I wouldn't want to do this with anyone but you.

Allison Zehnder

BIBLIOGRAPHY

1   "About Three-in-Ten U.S. Adults Are Now Religiously Unaffiliated." Pew Research Center. Web. Accessed 12 June 2024.

2   "Signs of Decline & Hope Among Key Metrics of Faith." Barna. Web. Accessed 12 June 2024.

3   Comer, John Mark. *Practicing the Way*. Waterbrook, 2024, p. 208.

4   Frank, Anne. *The Diary of Anne Frank*. Longman, 1989, Wednesday, October 7, 1942.

5   Frank, Anne. "Anne Frank Quotes." Goodreads. Web. Accessed 12 June 2024.

6   Cerullo, Megan. "More than half of college graduates are working in jobs that don't require degrees." CBS News. Web. Accessed 12 June 2024.

7   Delbanco, Andrew. *The Real American Dream*. Harvard University Press, 2009.

8   Mulvaney, Kieran. "The Stunning Survival Story of Ernest Shackleton and His Endurance Crew." History. Web. Accessed 12 June 2024.

9   Kessel, Michelle. "Melissa & Doug co-founder opens up about her secret struggle." CBS News. Web. Accessed 12 June 2024.

10 "List of accolades received by *The Shape of Water*." Wikipedia. Web. Accessed 12 June 2024.

11 Harrison, Spencer, Arne Carlsen and Miha Skerlavaj. "Marvel's Blockbuster Machine." Harvard Business Review. Web. Accessed 12 June 2024.

12 For a direct link to Gloria's episode on *The Red Letter Disciple Podcast* go to www.redletter-challenge.com/055.

13 Booth, Jessica. "Anxiety Statistics And Facts." Forbes. Web. Accessed 12 June 2024.

14 I am grateful to my friend Pastor Jeff Cloeter who initially wrote a blog that inspired much of the creativity behind this day. Jeff is a sixth-generation Lutheran pastor and you can read more about him at http://www.sixthgen.com/.

15 Luther, Martin. "Born to Us." Plough. Web. Accessed 12 June 2024.

16 Dal Bo, Ernesto, Pedro Dal Bo, and Jason Snyder. "Political Dynasties." The Review of Economic Studies. Web. Accessed 12 June 2024.

17 "Self Storage Trends and Statistics: 2024 Industry Report." Storeganise. Web. Accessed 12 June 2024.

18 Comer, John Mark. *The Ruthless Elimination of Hurry*. Waterbrook, 2019, p.144.

19 Lewis, C.S. *The Weight of Glory*. HarperCollins, 2001, p. 26.

20 Schrader, Jessica. "You're Not Laughing Enough, and That's No Joke." Psychology Today. Web. Accessed 12 June 2024.

21 Greatness Authors. "Laugh More, Live Longer: The Scientific Connection Between Laughter and Longevity." Greatness. Web. Accessed 12 June 2024.

22 Kinnaman, David, and Gabe Lyons. *UnChristian*. Baker Books, 2012, p. 26.

23 Pease, Glenn. "The Praise of Laughter." FaithWriters. Web. Accessed 12 June 2024.

24 Ibid.

25 I'm so grateful for Chris Burns, who helped creatively with today's devotion. Not only am I inspired by his great wisdom, but also by his example in life. Chris has built his life to help those in recovery. To find out more about Chris, go to www.rewrite-recovery.com.

26 Powell, Josh. "Turn Your Eyes Upon Jesus." Weapons of Grace. Web. Accessed 12 June 2024.

27 "Frankincense (carterii)." Alma Naturals Idaho. Web. Accessed 12 June 2024.

28 Khan, Akhtar J. "Medicinal properties of frankincense." International Journal of Nutrition, Pharmacology, Neurological Diseases. Web. Accessed 12 June 2024.

29 Groeschel, Craig. "The Gift, Part 1." Life.Church Open Network. Web. Accessed 12 June 2024.

30 "The Gift of the Magi-Myrrh." Three Magi. Web. Accessed 12 June 2024.

31 Frawley, Donna. "Frawley: many herbs we use today are featured in the Bible." Midland Daily News. Web. Accessed 12 June 2024.

32 Alcorn, Randy. "No One Was Happier Than Jesus." Desiring God. Web. Accessed 12 June 2024.

33 Keller, Timothy J. "Hidden Christmas Quotes." Goodreads. Web. Accessed 12 June 2024.

34 Green, Michael. "Unaware of His Possessions." Ministry 127. Web. Accessed 12 June 2024.

35 Pham, Tam. "You Can Make $15 Million Selling Pet Rocks." The Hustle. Web. Accessed 12 June 2024.

 FUN  INSPIRING  CRAZY  CHALLENGING

THE RED LETTER
DISCIPLE
WITH ZACH & CHRIS

The Red Letter Disciple is a podcast to help you become the greatest disciple of Jesus that you can possible be!

Learn more at:

WWW.REDLETTERPODCAST.COM

Subscribe or Follow:

Apple Podcasts

YouTube

Spotify

READY FOR
THE NEXT CHALLENGE?

40 DAYS TO BECOME A GREATER
DISCIPLE OF JESUS

EXPERIENCE RAPID GROWTH IN
YOUR RELATIONSHIP WITH GOD
IN ONLY 40 DAYS

EXPERIENCE THE FREEDOM OF
GOD IN JUST 40 DAYS!

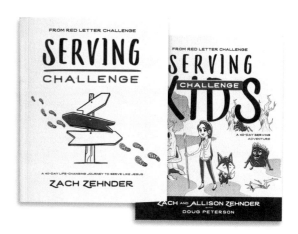

MAKE A LASTING DIFFERENCE IN
THE WORLD IN JUST 40 DAYS

FIND OUT MORE AT
WWW.REDLETTERCHALLENGE.COM

 FUN  INSPIRING  CRAZY  CHALLENGING

The Red Letter Disciple is a podcast to help you become the greatest disciple of Jesus that you can possible be!

Learn more at:

WWW.REDLETTERPODCAST.COM

Subscribe or Follow:

Apple
Podcasts

YouTube

Spotify

21 Greatness Authors. "Laugh More, Live Longer: The Scientific Connection Between Laughter and Longevity." Greatness. Web. Accessed 12 June 2024.

22 Kinnaman, David, and Gabe Lyons. *UnChristian*. Baker Books, 2012, p. 26.

23 Pease, Glenn. "The Praise of Laughter." FaithWriters. Web. Accessed 12 June 2024.

24 Ibid.

25 I'm so grateful for Chris Burns, who helped creatively with today's devotion. Not only am I inspired by his great wisdom, but also by his example in life. Chris has built his life to help those in recovery. To find out more about Chris, go to www.rewrite-recovery.com.

26 Powell, Josh. "Turn Your Eyes Upon Jesus." Weapons of Grace. Web. Accessed 12 June 2024.

27 "Frankincense (carterii)." Alma Naturals Idaho. Web. Accessed 12 June 2024.

28 Khan, Akhtar J. "Medicinal properties of frankincense." International Journal of Nutrition, Pharmacology, Neurological Diseases. Web. Accessed 12 June 2024.

29 Groeschel, Craig. "The Gift, Part 1." Life.Church Open Network. Web. Accessed 12 June 2024.

30 "The Gift of the Magi-Myrrh." Three Magi. Web. Accessed 12 June 2024.

31 Frawley, Donna. "Frawley: many herbs we use today are featured in the Bible." Midland Daily News. Web. Accessed 12 June 2024.

32 Alcorn, Randy. "No One Was Happier Than Jesus." Desiring God. Web. Accessed 12 June 2024.

33 Keller, Timothy J. "Hidden Christmas Quotes." Goodreads. Web. Accessed 12 June 2024.

34 Green, Michael. "Unaware of His Possessions." Ministry 127. Web. Accessed 12 June 2024.

35 Pham, Tam. "You Can Make $15 Million Selling Pet Rocks." The Hustle. Web. Accessed 12 June 2024.